D0580255

What a beautiful, tender, needed book—full of hope, understanding, wisdom and inspiration! I personally learned so much about how to fulfill my baptismal covenant to "mourn with those who mourn."

Dr. Stephen R. Covey,
author of *The 7 Habits of Highly Effective People*

Jesus Wept

Understanding & Enduring Loss

Coping with Death, Infertility and Miscarriage, Illness and
Disabilities, Divorce and Marital discord, Rebellious children,
Unwed pregnancy, Abuse, Same-gender attraction, Singleness,
Empty Nest Syndrome, Mid-life crisis, Homelessness,
and Unemployment.

Jesus Wept

Understanding & Enduring Loss

by

Joyce and Dennis Ashton

BONNEVILLE BOOKS™
Springville, Utah

Copyright © 2001 Joyce & Dennis Ashton

All Rights Reserved.

No part of this book may be reproduced in any form whatsoever, whether by graphic, visual, electronic, film, microfilm, tape recording, or any other means, without prior written permission of the author, except in the case of brief passages embodied in critical reviews and articles.

ISBN: 1-55517-562-7
v.4

Published by Bonneville Books
Imprint of Cedar Fort Inc.
www.cedarfort.com

Distributed by:

Typeset by Virginia Reeder
Cover design by Adam Ford
Cover design © 2001 by Lyle Mortimer

Printed in the United States of America
10 9 8 7 6 5 4 3 2 1

Printed on acid-free paper

 Library of Congress Cataloging-in-Publication Data
>
> Ashton, Joyce.
> Jesus wept : understanding & enduring loss / by Joyce and Dennis
> Ashton.
> p. cm.
> Includes bibliographical references and index.
> ISBN 1-55517-562-7 (pbk. : alk. paper)
> 1. Suffering--Religious aspects--Church of Jesus Christ of Latter-day
> Saints. 2. Loss (Psychology)--Religious aspects--Church of Jesus Christ
> of Latter-day Saints. 3. Church of Jesus Christ of Latter-day
> Saints--Doctrines. I. Ashton, Dennis, 1950- II. Title.
> BX8643.S93 A84 2001
> 248.8'6--dc21
>   2001003918

Dedication

In memory of Cameron Dale Ashton

Table of Contents

Preface

Many of the ideas for this work generated from our first book, entitled: *Loss and Grief Recovery*. It was written after Dennis and I lost a child at birth, two parents, and ultimately cared for and buried our fourteen year old son who was born with cerebral palsy. At the time we lived in the mission field and worked and associated with many non-members. *Loss and Grief Recovery* was written for an intended audience that represented many denominations. Over time we discovered that we were speaking and counseling with many Latter-Day Saints. We realized there were additional principles we wanted to share with those within the LDS church that our first book did not address. For example, our chapter on spiritual healing couldn't include Book of Mormon scriptures, quotes from modern-day prophets and other spiritual tools available to members.

We also discovered that virtually all of the serious challenges we experience in life have some form of loss at their root. We came to realize that death was not the only life trial that resulted in loss and grief, and that all of us will experience loss as we face varying degrees of adversity at different times throughout our life spans. Many losses will not be specifically mentioned. It is hoped that the reader can identify certain loss-and grief-recovery principles that may prove applicable to other loss issues.

Chapter one discusses general adversity and its effect on

LDS church members. Many of those facing adversity don't recognize that what they are experiencing is loss and grief. Others are at a loss as they attempt to help themselves. Chapters two through four provide opportunities for the reader to hear from members who have faced multiple kinds of loss. It provides insights into the challenges and suffering they endure. Chapters five to nine defines grief symptoms and offers interventions and self-help tools in five specific areas: physical, emotional, social, intellectual and spiritual. Chapter ten deals with some unique spiritual issues faced by Latter-Day Saints who lose a loved one. Chapters eleven and twelve provide helpful suggestions for coping with losses that impact and are often evident in marriage, children's grief, and parenting struggles. In chapter thirteen additional ideas are offered to assist caregivers and counselors in supporting others through the grief process. This book does not replace the need for professional counseling or medication.

Although both Dennis and I have authored this work, I will be the voice to make it easier to read.

Joyce Ashton

Acknowledgments

To the numerous clients, patients, friends and relatives who gave us permission to share their most intimate feelings, thoughts and pain.

SECTION I

LOSS AND GRIEF

INTRODUCTION TO OUR CRISIS

I had just settled into a nice, deep sleep when I heard the piercing sound of the telephone ringing. I glanced over at the clock, and as my eyes focused I could tell it was close to one a.m.. It was the hospital calling, the place I had just left, coming home to care for our children and get some needed rest. Dennis was spending the night at the hospital to be with our fourteen-year old son, Cameron, who had endured major surgery thirty-six hours earlier. The goal of the surgery was to re-tighten his hips which had started to dislocate due to his cerebral palsy. Although the first night following surgery brought a lot of pain, overall the doctors felt he had endured the procedure well. On Cameron's second day of recovery I had helped the nurse give him his bath, adjust his hip-spica cast, and pulled him around in a large wagon while she changed his bed. When Dennis arrived, we visited, going over the details of Cameron's care and our other children's schedules. I regret the last instructions I gave Dennis as I left the hospital. I had teasingly said, "Don't let him *code*!"—a term used to alert medical staff when a patient is near death.

The voice on the phone asked me to come back to the hospital. She said that Cameron wasn't doing well. I jumped from bed and started to get dressed. My first reaction was anger, as a nurse I knew the rules; one wasn't to tell family over the phone that their loved one had died, but to get them to the hospital safely first by telling them there had been a decline in their loved-one's health. I knew all too well what was going on and the probable fate I was about to be dealt. I remember yelling and throwing things around, saying, "It's not fair, not another death, not another trial, not another child gone!"

When I arrived at the hospital, the emergency room staff looked at me nervously. Soon a female doctor came out and knelt down in front of me. I braced myself for her message. This total stranger said four words to me: "Your son is dead!" Although I had suspected the worst, the words still came as a horrible shock. And even now, many years later, I feel the scorching pain of those four words. The doctor then led me to a little room where Cameron's lifeless body lay. He had tubes coming out from everywhere. Although, as a pediatric nurse, I had seen the same tubes and even put them in other children, they looked cold, frightening and cruel to me now. I saw, but felt no presence of our son, just his cold, lifeless shell. Alone and not knowing what to do, I kissed him on the forehead, and his familiar scent filled my nostrils. I then walked out in a state of numbness to find my husband. I found him alone, standing in the parking lot, in his own state of shock. He somehow felt responsible, that he had let Cam and I down. I sobbed on his shoulder, asking, "Why?" "Why"? Little did I know then it would take many years to finally reconcile this loss and find answers to those questions.

Dennis is a licensed psychotherapist. He has worked for twenty five years as a counselor, agency director, (and now assistant commissioner) with LDS Family Services. He has worked over the years with members and non-members who have suffered major losses in their lives. He has also worked with bereaved parents. However, he realized that night that he had not fully understood the degree of pain and depth of sorrow experienced by those he had counseled. He had

2

successfully helped others, but was now lost as to how to help himself.

In the course of our marriage we had faced a variety of losses; each bringing a new set of feelings and reactions. We suffered the death of a full-term baby, parents, grandparents, friends and relatives. We had also experienced other major losses including infertility, miscarriage, disabilities, life-threatening illness, rebellious children, difficult career relocations, demanding callings, and a serious fire that destroyed much of our home. We have also witnessed the suffering of close relatives as they endured suicide, marital discord, divorce, homosexuality, abuse, unemployment, singleness, cancer, midlife-and empty-nest syndrome. We realized now more completely that life's joys and triumphs are often accompanied with significant losses and pain. We began searching more earnestly for ways to help ourselves and others deal with adversity and find healing. We believed that our "Weeping may endure for a night, but joy cometh in the morning." (Psalm 30:5) We began our search for the promised joy.

We soon discovered that all of life's challenges have at their core some type of loss. (See Figure # 1) Most of life's disappointments and trials result from loss and will bear grief. In fact, one in every four individuals is experiencing some form of grief at any given moment. Our own journey through loss and grief has become our greatest teacher. Both of us have worked and served now for many years with hurting clients, friends and relatives. We would like to share the insights we and they have discovered as we journeyed together through the grief process.

CHAPTER I

"BAD THINGS HAPPEN TO GOOD PEOPLE" (1)

The scriptures remind us that "God sendeth rain on the just and the unjust and maketh his sun to rise on the evil and on the good." (3 Nephi 12:45, Matt 5:45) We've also heard the phrase "Life is what happens when you had other things planned."

Many members understand intellectually that bad things happen to good LDS people. However, when they actually experience a serious crisis firsthand, they struggle emotionally, finding it hard to believe that a significant tragedy has occurred to them. One struggling woman facing a serious personal crisis was told, "People of real faith don't have trials or crisis." One might imagine how that made her feel.

Members experiencing adversity often ask, "Why me?" "Where did I go wrong?" Others will reason, "I have faith, I live the Gospel, why am I struggling so much?"

In reality, bad things DO happen to good people, even worthy members of the church. Circumstances, often beyond our control, can result in pain and loss for both the righteous and the unrighteous. Some of us may think adversity affects only those who make poor choices, sin, lack sufficient faith, or are not wise enough to prevent or avoid adverse situations. We can bring trials upon ourselves; however, even when we are sincerely attempting to do everything the Lord would have us do, things can and do go astray. Marital discord, divorce, abuse, illness, death, disabilities, infertility, miscarriage, rebellious children, financial struggles, unemployment, homelessness, singleness, homosexuality, mid-life crisis, empty nest syndrome, or any unexpected change in life's expectations can bring feelings of pain, distress, sorrow, and despair.

Individuals experiencing severe grief seldom seem prepared to understand and successfully deal with all the emotions they are feeling. Some have been taught falsely, or have mistakenly understood that if they are righteous and faithful, they can avoid serious pain and loss in their lives. Others have believed that if something difficult happens to them, that their faith, obedience and prayer would protect or shield them from experiencing or FEELING serious emotional or physical pain. It may be especially confusing for those who have strong faith, believe in miracles and are striving to live the gospel, when they are not protected or shielded from serious adversity. Unfortunately, not even the righteous are granted all they desire or pray for. Many faithful individuals do not receive "the miracle" that they sincerely and desperately seek. Others endure pain as a result of the misuse of agency or poor choices of others.

Grief is immeasurable, difficult to describe, and often impossible to comprehend. The intensity of our grief can be correlated to the time invested, depth of our love, and the breadth of our relationship to the lost person, object or situation. The quality and quantity of our commitment and service, (emotional investment) often coincides with the difficulty and duration of our grief. Grief work will likely become the hardest work we will ever do. It will extract more time, patience and energy than most of us expect or feel capable of enduring.

"Grief cannot be compared, measured, or quantified...Healing...does not mean a quick cure; healing is putting the loss in perspective." (2 p. xiv)

No two individual's adjustment following a crisis will be

5

the same. Our reactions are as unique as our thumbprints. The type of loss is only one factor that affects our adjustment. Individual circumstances, former life experiences, and previous exposure to loss are a few of the other factors that contribute to our recovery process. (See figure # 2)

The Chinese symbol for "crisis" consists of two figures: danger and opportunity. Crisis and adversity provide us with opportunities to transform our pain into healing.

The following analogy is helpful when vexing the process of healing. I injured my knee snow skiing a few years ago. My knee has since healed; however, it has never quite been the same. Its vulnerability for re-injury has increased. Healing from my carpal tunnel surgery took about two years and, though much improved, my hand has never really been the same since. When we say we can heal from a tragic event or from a major loss which assaults both our body and soul, we need to remember that we will likely never be exactly the same again. Our loss becomes part of who we are, and although we can find joy and happiness again, we are forever different people.

Though many use the term "recovery" when referring to the grief process, professionals suggest that to "accommodate" may be a more accurate description of what most individuals experience. (3) Two additional concepts that more accurately describe this process are "adjustment and reconciliation". The Gospel assures me that I can anticipate full recovery for my knee and hand, as well as complete relief from any grief in the eternities!

Most members depend on their spiritual strength and religious beliefs to get them through difficult challenges. (See Chapter 9 on Spiritual healing) We are blessed to have the Gospel, and the gift of the Holy Ghost to comfort us. Christ offers us comfort and healing even when our adversity is not removed. While our faith and spiritual feelings bring great comfort, Dennis and I have also found it helpful to utilize and apply other therapeutic principles that facilitate the grief process. Just as I found splints, medication, surgery, and physical therapy helped my hand and knee, likewise therapeutic principles and healing interventions can help us accommodate or reconciliate our losses.

Accepting hardship is the first step in healing from any loss. (4) However, In the beginning or the acute phase, we may not have much control over our reactions and adjustment. As we acknowledge and actually pursue our "grief work", using faith and the tools discussed in the following chapters, we can gain increased control and peace. We will likely still experience grief attacks or grief bursts (just like I may re-sprain my knee). However, by exercising faith and doing our grief work, we are choosing to be a survivor rather than a victim of our circumstance.

Dennis and I quickly discovered that surviving our own personal crisis was more difficult than supporting others who were experiencing their losses. Most of us have not studied the impact of loss and grief in our formal education. In fact, we may have been conditioned to believe that others value us most when we deny our losses and appear capable and emotionally strong. As a result we choose to consciously hide (suppress) or subconsciously bury (repress) our painful or negative emotions. As church members we sometimes feel ashamed to openly admit our true feelings to ourselves or others. Unfortunately, when active members feel pain and loss and have a need to grieve, they sometimes choose to "mask" their true feelings, or shortcomings in order to save face. We may pretend to be functioning well in a desperate attempt to fool others and ourselves. This facade is reinforced when others compliment us with statements such as, "You are so strong and doing so well." Our desire not to disappoint others precludes us from sharing our true feelings and admitting we are struggling and need help. We then grieve in the shadows. This was explained well in a hospice newsletter:

"Whenever we doubt the legitimacy of our feelings, we begin to suppress ourselves and deny our own experience. In this way we inhibit our ability to recover from a loss, for allowing our feelings, whatever they may be, is essential to healing." (5)

There are many among us who have become silent sufferers. Some become inactive. They are afraid they will be judged negatively, especially if they feel somehow responsible for the adversity that they are enduring. This is often true of parents experiencing a rebellious child and couples going through divorce. Our guilt complicates the grieving process, causing us to feel shame and loss of control over our lives. Our grief becomes "disenfranchised" when no one allows, acknowledges or understands our loss. Consequently many of us suffer in silence, trying to make sense of our personal pain in private, and wonder if we are at fault, unworthy or responsible for our difficult circumstances, thinking, "Why am I having these feelings? I really must be a weak or bad person."

The wife of a prominent physician and church leader found it difficult to openly seek the help she needed following her husband's death. When he died, she said, "Everyone told me how strong I was, and how wonderfully I was handling his death." Initially she received a lot of support from family, friends and church members. Shortly thereafter she decided to serve a mission. When she returned home from her mission a concerned friend called LDS Family Services in her behalf. It was painful for her to admit many months later that she was still hurting and struggling as she continued to deal with the death of her husband. She was too ashamed to admit she needed help. She feared she would disappoint those who had commented on her strength if they discovered her seeking professional help after all these months. She did not realize her reactions to her husband's death were typical and that it can take many years to reconcile such a loss.

Unfortunately, this example is an all-too-common phenomena experienced by many church members as they contemplate seeking help from their church leaders, LDS Family Services or other health-care providers. Some choose nonmember counselors and practitioners to save face and avoid feeling judged. Others choose professional help offered by individuals who lack eternal perspectives rather than facing church members or leaders. Still others seeking help from LDS Family Services or other LDS therapists resist admitting to all the problems, stress, or adversity in their lives because they want to appear emotionally and spiritually strong.

If we look to the Savior for our example, we can find personal meaning in our losses. Christ is a "man of sorrows, and acquainted with grief. (Isaiah 53:3)

In John 11:35, we read two profound words: "Jesus wept."

The Savior was apparently not afraid to share emotion and grief with others who were mourning the loss of Lazarus. As they saw the Savior weep, some concluded: "...behold how he loved him" 11:36. "Jesus, therefore, again GROANING in himself cometh to the grave" 11:38. The Savior of the World openly expressed emotion in spite of knowing he could raise Lazarus or that his soul would live on.

Do we allow others and ourselves to openly express loss without judgment? Or do we hide from our grief, trying to ignore our pain and appear strong and faithful? Do we fear much like the following individual that it will somehow diminish the gospel message of hope if we acknowledge our true struggles and limitations? "I kept my fears and feelings to myself. What would the ward think of me if they knew I couldn't handle this?"

We have come to realize that when emotions resulting from loss are suppressed or repressed, they will eventually be expressed in some other form often resulting in serious distress in our physical, spiritual, and emotional lives. Serious mental illness also may result, leaving us unable to accomplish our grief work, or function fully at home, work, or church.

About eight months after the death of our son Cameron, I developed an eye twitch and some abnormal blood chemistry. Several doctors were unable to discover a cause or cure. Both conditions lasted about two years and then went away. Looking back I've realized that these physical ailments likely resulted from the impact of loss and grief on my body.

Grief work is hard work. It is the work of thoughts and feelings. In the beginning we often cannot choose or control the flood of emotions we experience. Over time most of us will have greater control and can decide how and when we'll grieve. Gaining emotional control will take longer than most of us expect or desire. We cannot make emotional injury go away any more than we can mend a broken leg with willpower alone.

"You cannot plant an acorn in the morning and expect that afternoon to sit in the shade of the oak." (6 p.58 Antoine De Saint-Excupery)

Recovery time will vary depending on multiple factors. Most individuals' recovery or adaptation will take from eighteen to twenty-four months following a traumatic loss. (7) Recovery time will be influenced by several factors including our emotional investment, the amount of grief work accomplished and additional factors indicated on Figure # 2 —*Coping Variables.*

Most individuals report fearing they will never be the same again following a major crisis. In reality they won't be! Their experience has become a part of them and has forever changed how they look at the world and themselves. They can, however, adapt to their loss, as they discover their "New Normal"(2 p.xv) and realize peace and "joy cometh in the morning". (Psalm 30:5)

In the Bible we see forcefully illustrated the life-changing result of a major loss in the account of Jacob and his twelve sons. Jacob was led to believe his favorite son, Joseph, had died after his other eleven sons staged his death and sold him to the Egyptians. Jacob experienced intense grief.

"And Jacob rent his clothes and put sackcloth upon his loins and mourned for his son many days. And all his sons and all his daughters rose up to comfort him, but he refused to be comforted.

"For I will go down into the grave unto my son, mourning. Thus his father WEPT for him." (Genesis 37:34-35)

Jacob outwardly displayed his grief and acknowledged that he would always miss his son. He realized he would not be able to enjoy his son's company and association on earth. He wouldn't see him marry and bear grandchildren. Expectations of how he thought his life would be, his assumptive world, were altered. Jacob felt initially that he would never get "over" his loss. Eventually he did get "through" his loss by adjusting to his new circumstances. We know he went on to live a long and abundant life full of joy and adversity.

Later when he was told that Benjamin must go down to Egypt, he displayed his vulnerability and fear concerning the possibility of experiencing another major loss.

". . . Ye know my wife (Rebecca) bare me two sons: (Joseph and Benjamin) And the one (Joseph) went out from me, and I said, Surely he is torn in pieces; and I saw him not since: And if ye take this (Benjamin) also from me, and mischief befall him, ye shall bring down my gray hairs with sorrow to the grave." (Genesis 44:27-29)

The accumulative impact of Jacob's multiple losses complicated his grief process. Nevertheless, adaptation or recovery is possible. We can find joy and happiness again. (Psalms 50:5) However, for many it will follow a long and difficult journey.

CHANGE AND LOSS

Adversity and loss are usually the result of life's changing circumstances and expectations. Any major alteration in one's life can result in feelings of loss and grief requiring transition and resolution.(8 p.1) Changes in living conditions, location, status, employment, health, appearance, weight, responsibility, stewardships, etc. can all produce feelings of loss and give birth to a need to grieve. (9). Many believe that we can only lose what we have once had. Some, however, will grieve over hopes and dreams that were never fully realized or completely fulfilled. Those who never marry or who never bare children often experience this kind of grief. It can also be felt by children who have been abused or unloved. A friend raised by an emotionally disabled mother shared, "I grieve for the love my mother couldn't give me." This friend, like many other individuals, are born into or inherit their loss, similar to children who are orphaned, abandoned or raised in poverty and despair.

"We experience losses throughout our lives; separation, divorce transitions, all kinds of changes, yet our culture has not prepared us well to deal with them... This world is not reality. It takes a brave soul with an adventurous outlook to prepare for the inevitable losses that are to come." (10 p. 13)

The following three chapters contain a number of common losses. They primarily focus on the personal experiences and feelings of church members enduring adversity. The purpose of these chapters is to help us identify with and understand the challenges others are experiencing as they deal with their feelings of loss and grief. These chapters are also designed to help us normalize our own loss and grief symptoms as we realize we are not grieving alone. It is not possible to specifically mention every conceivable human loss; however, it is hoped that the reader can identify grief-recovery principles that may prove applicable to numerous loss issues. Keep in mind that what may be a crisis for one person may not be for another.

Also remember that we are entering the private world of another's adversity. Please enter with compassion, empathy, and a nonjudgmental attitude, remembering our baptismal covenant to "mourn with those that mourn" (Mosiah 18:9).

CHAPTER 2

MEMBERS DISCUSS THEIR LOSS FOLLOWING THE DEATH OF A LOVED ONE, MURDER AND SUICIDE, INFERTILITY AND MISCARRIAGE

More than two million individuals die in the US every year. The family support offered to the bereaved in the past has been eroded due to our mobility and age-segregated living arrangements. Consequently, many people grieve alone. The death of a loved one may result in a major loss and crisis.

The death of a parent is considered a loss of our past. The death of a spouse constitutes the loss of our present. The death of a child represents the loss of our dreams for the future.

As grief counselors, Dennis and I discourage individuals from comparing the severity of their loss to others. It is difficult to judge how intense another person feels about the same loss we are experiencing. There are just too many individualized factors (See figure #2). However, we can compare the individual impact of our own losses. For example, when Dennis and I put our losses on a scale (see figure #1) of one to ten with ten being the most intense loss, we listed the death of our grandparents as "1," our miscarriage as "2," moves and financial struggles as "3," the death of our parents as "4" (including a suicide), infertility and house fire as "5," and the death of our baby and birth of a disabled child as "6."

In contrast to those losses, "10" doesn't seem high enough on the loss scale to account for the extreme pain both of us experienced following the death of our fourteen-year old son. The impact of his death seemed several times the magnitude of anything we had previously experienced.

Dennis spent a month in Albania evaluating the Kosovo refugee situation for LDS Family Services and the Church Humanitarian Department. The experience made him question how *we* would cope if faced with the multiple losses that these people were enduring. They had lost land, home, possessions, employment, and comfort. They experienced and witnessed illness and the death of friends and loved ones. Their numerous losses were further complicated by the cruelty, purposelessness, and randomness of these senseless murders. (See *Murder* on p. 21)

LOSS OF A SPOUSE

Some professionals feel there is more social support available following the loss of a spouse. Nevertheless, losing one's best friend, lover and life companion leaves many lost, lonely and heavy hearted. Even though we realize that one of us must go first, it is no easy task to say good-bye.

Widowers usually display less emotional grief and have more trouble adapting to practical problems, such as housework and child care. Widows conversely usually experience a sense of abandonment and require more support with their emotional issues.

The most common complaint expressed to me as a hospice worker is the LONELINESS felt following the loss of a spouse.

One woman said after the death of her husband:

"It is so hard. I need help. I am falling apart. I am not coping. I don't know what to do."

Another widow was asked by friends:

"What can we do to help you?" Her reply was, "Undo it!"

A man who lost his wife said:

"My wife was so healthy when she suddenly got ill and died. I am still in shock to be left alone so suddenly. I go over and over the details of her death. I am so emotional."

We often struggle to understand and say the right things. Our attempt to give advice rather than listen and empathize can cause additional pain and loss: A sister in one of our wards lost her husband and son in the same accident. The Relief Society president said to the her, "Well, some people lose their whole family; at least you have your daughter." This mother was angered by the statement and became inactive for years. She turned her anger toward the church because a well-meaning member and church representative made a hurtful statement.

Another widow who had cared for her ill husband for many years was told:

"You should be glad, now you can have a life."

Many don't understand that caring for someone so intensely often deepens our bond with them, complicating or intensifying our loss. It's normal to feel relief from the hard work of caring for a loved one and watching them suffer; however, we will still mourn and miss them.

Another widow after losing her husband was told:

"I know just how you feel, my dog died last week."

The loss of a pet can be a major loss for some; however, it may hurt others whenever we make such comparisons. (See *More Cliches* p. 234; and *Loss of Pets* p. 216)

DEATH OF A PARENT

Twelve million Americans will bury a parent this year. Unfortunately the grieving of adult children is often disenfranchised. Because society expects and accepts the loss of older parents, their children's grief often goes unrecognized. However, the death of a parent can be difficult at any age.

Young children often struggle as they attempt to make sense of a loss they can't developmentally understand. Many children also experience a sense of abandonment after the death of a parent which may cause serious anxiety or even panic attacks.

A young girl who lost her mother said:

"I know that I should be happy. She's well in heaven. But I miss her so!" What relief she felt when she learned it was okay and normal to miss her mother and feel sad. She needed permission to grieve.

A twenty one-year-old woman said:

"My mother died after years of suffering. I felt relieved that her suffering had ended."

My own mother tells this story:

"My parents died when I was fourteen, eight months apart. I would go in the coat closet and put on my mother's fur coat and weep. The smell and warmth made me feel close to her."

I wrote the following after my father died:

"I couldn't sleep for two weeks after my father died. I couldn't understand how my mother could sleep in the same bed where he died. I could hardly walk past the bedroom. It was so frightening for me."

When Dennis's mother died he said:

"After my mother committed suicide, the hardest part for me was watching the pain of my father and knowing my younger brothers would be raised without a mother."

LOSS OF A SIBLING

Loss of a sibling can be very confusing for young children as well as adult survivors. It's common for the bereaved parents to canonize the deceased child and for other siblings to feel unloved or that their parents love their deceased sibling more:

"After my brother died, my husband tried to comfort me with, "Well, we know he is okay where he is." Later, my mom felt really cut off spiritually and was a little upset because everybody else was getting dreams, impressions and feelings, and she was in a "black hole," so to speak. My Dad went off the "deep end," in my opinion...My deceased brother was always visiting with him and letting him know that things were right or wrong. My sister and I perceived continual slights from our parents, especially when a letter went out to hundreds of friends and relatives titled: 'The Joy of our Life is Gone.' After being so certain of my Heavenly Father and His plan, I hardened my heart and refused to believe for a long time."

Another sibling reminds us of the need to be sensitive: "Soon after my brother died my visiting teacher kept asking if and when my sister-in-law would re-marry. This upset me and really hurt my feelings."

A sibling writes:
"When my parents start getting down about the death of my brother, I usually leave the room. I just can't talk to them about him. I don't know how to talk to them. I feel like no matter what I say it comes out wrong and hurts them. I'm not good at saying what I mean. I'm afraid to cry about the death of my brother because it might upset them more. I cry alone most of the time. I can talk to my sister."

After Cameron died, one of our sons said,

"I feel guilty that I hadn't been a better brother. I should have been kinder to him."

We will discuss how to help grieving children in Chapter Twelve.

LOSS OF A CHILD

"The death of a child is the most traumatic event in a parent's life." (1)

For many years Dennis and I worked with parents who had lost children. However, we had no idea that their suffering and pain was so intense until we lost our own child. We were shocked at the magnitude of our grief. We discovered that it is difficult to understand what someone else is going through without experiencing it ourselves. Even then we must avoid saying that we know how someone feels, because each individual and circumstance is different (See Figure #2). The following excerpts are from parents in a support group who have lost a child:

"When my son died I felt like half of me was ripped away. I felt like all my hopes and dreams, as well as my child, had been taken away."

"I can still feel today the absolute cold feeling of my son's skin as I kissed him goodbye on the forehead. That will be with me forever as a reminder that he was taken from us so suddenly, and represents the feeling of absence and loss that weigh upon us."

"My heart literally aches. I miss him so much. I'm still numb. I fear the quiet of our house."

"I miss watching her jump on the trampoline. She always wanted me to spot her. I also miss my old life and how my wife was before this tragedy. We can never be the same."

"It has been almost twenty years since the car accident of our three-year-old son. I know I will be with him in the Celestial Kingdom; however, I still miss him and wish I could have raised him on earth. Our grief was very intense at first. It almost cost us our marriage. Our grief has turned into mourning, which seems to be staying with us a lifetime."

Professionals are now suggesting that "Accommodation as contrast to recovery captures more accurately the process that most individuals experience following a major loss. Major losses can be integrated into the rest of life; however, final closure usually cannot be obtained and is not even desirable." (2 p.221)

An example of this reality is evident in the account of a mother whose child died forty years ago. She recently ran into her deceased daughter's best friend shopping with her grand-daughter. This mother experienced a grief attack, mourning again as she realized she had missed forty years without her daughter, and now is also missing her role as grandmother to a lost generation of grandchildren! This account illustrates secondary losses and the developmental aspects of grief. (3)

After Cameron died, Dennis said:
"I had been in the counseling field for fifteen years when Cameron died. I had worked with many individuals who had experienced loss, even the loss of children. However, when it happened to me I was knocked down hard. It is the only time

in my life of many losses (infant, fire, financial, grandparents, mother's suicide) that I couldn't immediately get up. I was at a loss at first as to how I could help myself. After several years I realized that I had adjusted and accommodated to my loss, but I also realized I would never fully recover from the impact of Cameron's death on my life."

Two mothers discuss their pain:

"The loss of my child is something that is hard to put into words. I had no clue that this kind of pain existed in the world. I don't think anyone can understand unless they've 'been there'. I wish I wasn't 'here'. My life will never be the same. I'm trying not to become bitter because I feel I have been robbed of so much happiness."

"We lost our only daughter and youngest child on her birthday. We are barely holding on."

MURDER

Murder is a serious transgression. It abuses one's agency and shortens the victims life's experiences and probation time (See *A Time to Die*, p. 187). Those who lose a loved one to murder not only have to deal with the loss of their loved one, but the traumatic way they died, and the judicial system. It can impair one's sense of safety and trust. Combined, these factors can complicate and prolong the grieving process, making it difficult for some to function again at home, work, church or in society.

A woman approached us after we spoke at a bereavement conference and said:

"A few years after the death of my husband, my daughter was murdered. I am the one who found her battered body in her apartment. Words cannot describe the intense trauma, pain, loss and anger that I feel. I felt I had pretty much recovered from my husband's death when my daughter died. However, I can't seem to recover from this one. It's been five years now and I am still in therapy."

Death caused at the hand of a murderer becomes complicated because it could have been prevented. One feels intensely violated when someone purposely takes the life of their loved one.

A mother whose daughter was raped and murdered said: "It's been seven years...You never forget it, you just learn to live with the pain. It's something you just don't get over." (4 p.169)

SUICIDE

Those who take their own lives are usually in tremendous mental, emotional or physical pain. Remember that God is their judge—we may not understand all the dynamics associated with these acts. Those left behind struggle with many questions, confusion and guilt, wondering "Could I have done something that would have made a difference?"

Their mourning processes can become complicated and prolonged as with murder.

Bruce R. McConkie taught: "...persons subject to great stresses may lose control of themselves and become mentally clouded to the point that they are no longer accountable for their acts. Such are not to be condemned for taking their own lives. It should also be remembered that judgement is the Lord's;... and he in his infinite wisdom will make all things right in due course." (5, p.711)

Each year in the U.S. there are over thirty thousand suicides reported to the Centers for Disease Control and Prevention. Imagine the intense pain experienced by multiple numbers of family and friends mourning these losses. Included amid those reported deaths were four children under nine years of age! More than five hundred thousand adolescents and the same number of adults attempt suicide annually. Five to six thousand teens succeed and five times that number of adults die annually. Suicide is the fifth cause of death among five to fourteen-year-olds. (6, p. 186)

Depression can lead to suicide (See p. 69). Often the depressive symptoms go unrecognized, especially in children and teens. Others won't admit they have a problem and refuse medication, often for fear of appearing weak.

Dennis's mother committed suicide on her fiftieth birthday. She left a distraught husband and two young sons still at home. Incidents in her life history had contributed to her depression and suicide. Her mother moved out of the home at an early age. She quit school in the eighth grade to help raise her younger siblings and care for their home. Her father died at a young age. Ultimately, she experienced serious panic attacks and developed other significant health problems. Her addiction to alcohol and prescription drugs eventually intensified her feelings of frustration and hopelessness.

M. Russell Ballard writes:

"The act of taking one's life is truly a tragedy because this single act leaves so many victims: first the one who dies, then the dozens of others—family and friends—who are left behind, some to face years of deep pain and confusion." (7, p.8-9)

"My nephew very much wanted to serve a mission. He tried on two occasions to stay at the MTC. His depression overcame him and he returned home discouraged both times. Soon after, he committed suicide. We are all devastated."

A woman in my bereavement group was struggling as she tried to cope with the death of both of her children. Her oldest son had died of cancer. On the first anniversary of his death, her daughter, who was still grieving his death, committed suicide. Following such a devastating loss, she said:

"The pain and sadness is just too much for me to handle. I really would like to join my children in the Spirit World. I think about it a lot."

Other bereaved parents have stated to us years after their losses that they were surprised to still be alive; however, they felt proud to have made it through!

Guilt is a common emotion for those siblings left behind:
"My brother's last words to me were, "Help me". Three weeks later he committed suicide. I was left haunted. Haunted by my failure as a sister to save my only sibling's life. Haunted, too, by a wide range of emotions, which I chose to bury for twenty seven years. I have been frozen in the grief process." (8)

It's important to know that once someone has made up their mind to take their life, no amount of talking, interventions or effort on our part alone will guarantee that they will not attempt suicide. Every threat and suicidal gesture must be considered valid and potentially lethal.

Anyone who has lost a loved one may find comfort in Chapter Ten on *Death and Spirituality.*

INFERTILITY / MISCARRIAGE / NEONATAL LOSS

Few understand the frustration, loss and pain of infertility and neonatal loss. It took Dennis and I a few years to become pregnant. Each month seemed like an eternity. When I finally conceived we were thrilled. After nine and a half long months labor began: "We had tried for two years to have a child. Now I was two weeks over my due date, and I knew any minute now I would be holding a baby! During the night I had several contractions off and on. The baby's movements had slowed down during contractions, in fact I thought it had been a long time since I had felt her move at all. My mother called an OB nurse she knew at the hospital. Although she tried to reassure us that sometimes babies do slow down and move less during labor, she said to come into the hospital right away. Fear gripped us as we anticipated something might be wrong with our baby. We decided to pray before we left for the hospital. I was disappointed in Dennis's words because there was no promise of a live, healthy baby. When we arrived, no heartbeat could be found. When the doctor broke my water it was green, a sign of fetal distress. I said, "Just put me to sleep and take it out!" The doctor explained it would be best for me to endure the labor and deliver her vaginally. A few hours later after much pain and pushing, I delivered a beautiful baby girl, almost seven pounds. She looked perfect. However, she was stillborn! A reason for her death was never determined. I was in shock for days!" (9 Chp.14 p.4)

A woman from my neonatal loss support group writes:
"We were so thrilled to finally be pregnant! We had been in and out of fertility clinics for five years. We had finally conceived through IUI (intro-uterine insemination). We were nineteen weeks along and went in for our usual check up. The

doctor sent us for a routine ultrasound which showed that our baby had died! We couldn't believe it! The previous week the baby had a strong heartbeat! How did this happen? Everyone around us was having children. Why us? I was in shock for days! As I anticipated being induced to deliver my baby, I still wasn't sure it was all happening. Even after delivery, I thought I could still feel the baby moving. It took a long time for me to believe I had lost my baby. My grief lasted for over a year. Most people didn't seem to understand. They claimed I never knew my child, who wasn't even born yet, so why was my grief so long and so hard? I really didn't feel happy again until I was pregnant and finally delivered a healthy baby. And even now I wish I had both babies!"

A grieving young woman writes:
"I had three ectopic pregnancies. The first one destroyed my right tube, and the third one my left. The hardest part is knowing I cannot conceive again. I always just wanted to stay home and be a mom. Now I have to replan my life. I cry a lot."

An infertile woman writes:
"I am forty years old and had been trying for years to conceive. When I finally got pregnant, we were thrilled! We told everyone, and celebrated by buying maternity clothes. Although I only was pregnant a few weeks, I had planned my whole life around this baby. My life was shattered when I miscarried. No one could understand why I was so devastated because I had just found out I was pregnant. My time is running out and I wonder if I will ever be a mother." (9, Chp. 14, p.3)

A grieving mother was told by a well-meaning friend that God needed and wanted her baby; she responded, "God has lots of babies, we only had one." Many well-meaning individuals try to discount the importance of losing a baby: A grieving mother, after losing triplets and following years of infertility, was told by her sister: "I've gotten over the loss of your babies, but I'm still grieving for Grandma." This mother was hurt and thought to herself, "It is much easier to get over the loss of someone else's babies. The grief I felt at Grandma's anticipated death following her long, fruitful earth life is small when compared to the loss of my three babies. The reality that I may never be a mother in this life destroys both my present and future hopes and dreams!"

Enduring Mothers-or Fathers Day after a loss of a child is very difficult. Dennis and I remember clearly our first Mother's Day after losing our first baby. We attended church and I was sitting in front of the congregation with the group of primary children I taught. They had sung a Mother's Day song and now the ward was going to pass out flowers to all the moms. The announcement was made for all the mothers to stand. I knew I was a mother, however, I wasn't sure if others knew. I decided not to stand up. I could feel the tears welling up in my eyes. I felt the whole audience was staring at me. (I wished I wasn't sitting up in front!) I felt so sad and it was so hard to keep my emotions in check. The flowers were almost all passed out, my heart was pounding. As the last mother sat down, some kind soul must have whispered and cued the young boy walking toward me with a flower outstretched. I gratefully took the flower and felt relieved. I felt someone had recognized not only my motherhood, but also my grief.

SUBSEQUENT PREGNANCY

Expectant parents who have recently experienced a neonatal loss can become vulnerable and circumspect. The process of bonding and attaching with children that follow may be delayed and sometimes distorted.

"I was born soon after my mother lost a baby. I have realized that my parents struggle to attach to me was compromised by their fear of losing another child. I think my parents kept me at a distance."

Others attempting to deal with their fears and vulnerability may become overprotective of their child. After our first baby's death, each pregnancy was filled with fear of a subsequent death or other serious loss. I wanted to wear a monitor to check the baby's heart rate around the clock! After Cameron died, we became overly concerned that our other children might be seriously injured or killed. Every time they wanted to use the car, fear would grip us. When anyone came home late, my mind would race through all the frightening possibilities. This feeling of vulnerability and worrying about what else might happen was exhausting. Fortunately, as the grief process progressed we felt more secure and peaceful.

CHAPTER 3

MEMBERS DISCUSS THEIR LOSS FOLLOWING ILLNESS AND DISABILITIES, DIVORCE AND MARITAL DISCORD, RAISING REBELLIOUS CHILDREN, AND UNWED PARENTS.

ILLNESS AND DISABILITIES

A diagnosis of serious illness or disability spawns difficult adjustments for individuals, married couples and families. Watching someone suffering expands our understanding as we realize that we may grieve for the living as well as the dead. Some individuals suffering significant physical or emotional pain report that they would rather die than continue to endure their suffering. Those watching at the bedside as caregivers may feel similarly.

A few years ago I experienced firsthand the fear and helplessness that those who become seriously ill or disabled must endure. I woke up in the middle of the night and could not move the left side of my body. Panic seized me—I wondered if I was having a heart attack, like the one that ended my father's life at age sixty two. I woke Dennis and asked him to call 9-1-1 and to give me a blessing. After a few days in the hospital the doctors decided I'd had a TIA or mini-stroke. I had a full recovery; however, now my physician has discovered brain lesions indicative of Multiple Sclerosis. I'm left wondering what will become of my health and my future ability to function normally.

A daughter whose mother died of cancer said: "My

mother's breast cancer returned after many years of remission. She refused to do the chemotherapy again. She died within a few months. I am hurt and angry that she wouldn't try to survive for her family."

A young cancer survivor said:
"My cancer experience left me emotionally drained and severely depressed. There were times it was more than I could bare, and I wanted to die. If my cancer returns I will not go through all the treatments again. I will just take pain medication until I die. I am not afraid of physical pain, it's the emotional pain that I cannot do again."

Disease can literally put a person in a state of "dis-ease".
Eight million people are living today with a history of cancer. An additional 1.2 million will be diagnosed with the disease this year alone. (1)

A woman from my breast cancer support group shared: "I lost all my hair during chemotherapy. Sometimes I would take my wig off and swing it around, being silly. One of my children would laugh, but the other would ask me to please not do it."

Before I started working directly with individuals with serious illness, I had expected to see some type of chronic sorrow or depression. However, reactions are, in fact, very individualized. Each new day introduces a new set of emotions. These emotions are influenced by medical treatments, test results, and current health status. Individual's reactions are also influenced and weighted against the quality and anticipated duration of life. For many, the constant ups and downs of remissions and relapses is exhausting.

"My son relapsed after the bone marrow transplant. We were told all that could be done had been done. I felt such guilt for what I had put him through all these months. There were blood tests, bone marrow aspirations, spinal taps, radiation and chemotherapy that made him so sick. I was with him through them all. They were difficult to watch. Now after all he's been through, it didn't work anyway, I am angry, nervous, uneasy and totally devastated." (2 Chp.14 p.7)

"When I was given the initial diagnosis of leukemia by our pediatrician, I felt like I was in a huge hole, trying to keep my composure so I could call my husband. When the diagnosis was confirmed by specialists, I was overcome with hopelessness and dread."

There are few situations worse than watching helplessly as someone you love suffers.

"I felt like my chest was going to cave in, it hurt so badly. I wanted to protect my child from any pain she might experience. I couldn't believe she was going to have to go through this."

"When my mother told me about her cancer I was twelve years old. I was so upset. I ran to my friend's house crying all the way! I just knew she would immediately die. This experience hearing of mother's diagnosis was more difficult for me than her death seven years later."

Receiving the diagnosis of a disability can also begin the grief process.

"My child could see normally for many years and had many friends in and out of the church. After she lost her vision she also lost her friends. It became very difficult for both of us."

"When you get pregnant, it's like planning a fabulous trip to a place you've dreamed of all your life, maybe...to Italy. You buy a bunch of guide books and make wonderful plans. It's all very exciting. After months of eager anticipation, the day finally arrives. You pack your bags and off you go. Several hours later, the plane lands. The stewardess says, "Welcome to Holland." "What!? I signed up for Italy....I've wanted to go there all my life! "Well there's been a change in the flight plan, and here you must stay! It's not a horrible place, just different than you expected. You must learn a different language. And everyone you know is talking about their trip to Italy, and how wonderful it is there. "Yes," you say, "I was supposed to go there too." The pain of this change will never go away, the loss of the dream. "I will try and see the beautiful things in Holland. They do have tulips and windmills!" (3)

I wrote of my own struggle of going out in public with our son, Cameron, who had cerebral palsy:
"People often stared at the wheelchair. I think I could sometimes feel their pity. Other times I worried I might offend someone by bringing him out in public to eat. It was difficult to help him eat, and my other children seemed impatient, as well as my nursing baby!"

There are often secondary losses that effect and shape our lives:
"I've spent most of my life working hard to get good grades and a good career. I married and started my family before I finished law school. I finally got a job offer with the company of my dreams; however, I couldn't accept it due to the serious illness and disabilities of my child."

I wrote the following in my journal when Cam was in kindergarten:

"I have been helping Cameron in his classroom. I worry when I see him with the other normal children. He doesn't fit in very well. It's very sad and emotional for me to watch. It's hard at home, too; lifting, feeding and bathing him. I get feeling down and discouraged and sometimes I ask God why. One day Cameron angrily asked me, 'Why am I handicapped anyway?' I said, 'It's our challenge.' He said, 'I want to be normal. I want to walk, I want to walk!' I tried to comfort him. However, sometimes I'm not sure how to help him. I often feel sad for him and for me."

A new mother writes after hearing the terminal diagnosis of her newborn baby:

"I could not stop crying, except at night when I was sometimes asleep. I just could not believe that she would experience pain, breathing difficulties and eventually die!"

Another mother, after finding little support during her son's illness, became totally immersed in the work of caring for her child, unable to attend to little else:

"I am the main caregiver. My husband doesn't really do much of the necessary care. He has thrown himself into his work and earning the money to enable me to stay at home. This has caused some arguments because if he would give some of the medications, or treatments I could have a break, or eat hot food!" (4 p.26)

A mother with a disabled child writes:

"My doctor has said he wished there was a group of parents that could trade babysitting duties. When I think of that it scares me because I just don't know if they could take care of my ill child the way I do. Most of the time I feel I'm the only one that can do it. This is hard because it allows me no time for myself. Each time I've started an exercise class, he gets sicker and I feel I have to quit going." (4 p.26)

When Cameron was born we felt responsible for his physical, spiritual, social and emotional care and growth. How would everyone accept this less-than-"normal" child? How could we help him accept himself in spite of his limitations? We wanted to give Cameron every opportunity available. Like most parents we wanted to insure that he had the opportunity to be the best that he could be. The professionals could not tell for sure if he would ever walk, so we worked long and hard assuming he would. It took many years for us to realize that he would not. We learned that his growth would be a slow process, and that small accomplishments would measure Cameron's success and progress. The doctor did feel that Cameron would not be able to talk, so we helped teach him how to use a communication board. He learned to use it very fast, and then surprised us when he began speaking. I wrote the following the first time he said more than one word at a time:

"Cameron's first partial sentence was a small miracle to us. He was three years old and this was the first day that he would go to a special preschool without Mom, all alone on a bus. As I was dressing him I could see the anxiety in his eyes. His big brown eyes always melted my heart. He looked up at me and asked, 'Mamma go?' Tears came to my eyes and I cheered, 'You spoke, you spoke!' With great emotion I explained he would be going to school alone, but I would be home when he returned. We were going to have some great communication together and make the most of his limitations!

He had communicated and I had understood! This was such a great thrill!"

It wasn't long before Cameron's slurred speech replaced his need to use the communication board. We were all thrilled and grateful that he could be understood eventually by many at home, church, and school.

Other parents will bear children who may never speak with words. These parents may need to look deeper for positive qualities within their children's personalities and spirits. If they are able to focus on their child's inner qualities (self-worth) and the importance of their child's existence as a child of God, ("being" not "doing") they will find meaning and purpose. (See p. 107, 228 on self-esteem.)

Over the years we had learned to accept Cameron's disability and love him intensely. Although it was hard work, we found joy and purpose in caring for him. We spent nearly every day for fourteen years feeding, bathing, and dressing him and addressing his medical and emotional needs. He attended special schools and endured hours of the physical, occupation, and speech therapy. He was happy and loved living. We spent countless hours trying to find the right wheelchair, computer, typewriter, electric bed, prone standing table, eating utensils and school programs.

Six months before his death, Cameron expressed the following ideas and feelings to a class of college students majoring in special education. It took an hour to videotape Cameron's fourteen-minute testimony, due to his labored speech and limited grammar:

"Hi! ... It not easy being different (he was realistic). It look easy, but not really. It like hard, I guess. Like for example, I can't do a lot. But I can play with my computer, and I hope to learn more about the computer so I can teach my mom and dad to use it and stuff (He looks for the positive). I hope you understand me okay, and can learn what it like to be me (He was concerned for others). It's fun to ride my bike and wheelchair, it's like walking for me. I can swim with a little help from this (holds up some arm floats. His focus is on the things he *can* do). I have a trampoline, it over there (points), and I can jump on it, I mean I can lay on it and have somebody jump with me (He's honest). My family is really nice. My dad helps me get dressed in the morning and helps me go bathroom and all that. I have aide who helps me work good at school.(He feels appreciation to others). Here my suggestions to you college helpers. Be nice to handicapped kids because it hurt their feelings (sensitivity). I really feel that I can walk in the next life, and that I can talk better (His faith and hope). And that I live forever in the next life after this and that I will see God again (His belief in a God and a next life). And I get to see my Grandma and Grandpa who died a couple years ago, again. And you can too someday. I guess I don't have to say anymore. And this is Cameron signing off. (His humor!) (4 p.64)

When he died we felt devastated and lost.

DIVORCE

The death of a marriage is painful, lonely and complex. There are usually no funeral services, sympathy cards, condolence calls, or flowers sent. Divorce can affect one's personality and identity in dramatic and damaging ways. (5)

Divorce is especially devastating if you've grown up in the church believing that someday, if you're worthy, you can be married "forever". Establishing an eternal family is the hope and dream of many wonderful young couples. Fortunately we do have many wonderful marriages and families in the church where everyone works together to realize these promises.

Unfortunately there are others whose dreams are shattered in spite of their wholehearted and righteous efforts.

"All my hopes, dreams and energy have gone toward my temple marriage and my children. I am still in shock that it is gone. It came down to a decision I had to make. How did this happen?"

We watched helplessly one year as a close friend, relative, and our bishop's wife were all left by their spouses during the same time period. A total of sixteen children lost a parent in these three homes. Divorce for these members was viewed as an "eternal loss" because of the catastrophic consequences that extend beyond earth life. We comfort those who have lost a loved one to death by reassuring them that they will eventually see, hold and love their deceased loved one in the eternities. How do we comfort men and women who have lost an eternal mate to divorce? They may no longer be part of the "forever" family they loved, sacrificed for, and planned to spend eternities with.

"I am a thirty nine-year old woman with several children still at home. I grew up in the church, married a returned missionary in the temple after fasting and praying to confirm my decision. My husband and I have always been worthy and active in the church. Last year my husband told me he didn't love me any more and wanted a separation and probably a divorce.

"I was overcome with shock and confusion. How could this happen? I feel so helpless and hopeless. I have prayed, fasted, attended the temple begging for God's help. I pray that my husband will return, or that I can find some permanent peace and resolution. Neither has occurred yet. I feel I am worthy and have faith for a miracle. I have done everything possible to ensure a good life and a temple marriage.

"I don't feel as comfortable at church. I feel everyone is looking at me, feeling sorry for me, or wondering what I did to drive my husband away. The sacrament talks and lessons in Relief Society do not offer much comfort right now.

"My husband has told me he cannot afford to pay for two places to live, so I must look for work. I'm not sure I am capable of so much stress right now. What will my children do? How will they cope with their father leaving, and now me going to work? What has happened to my eternal family? It's hard to want to go on when the most important thing to me is gone."

How can we support those in the church who have experienced an eternal loss? We believe God is just and will compensate for the pain these parents and children feel. These three women all wanted the husbands they were sealed to in the temple. They were willing to forgive and forget; however, each husband was choosing something else. These women all lost the person they had planned and committed to spend earth life and eternity with. They all have told us they don't want to have to learn to love someone else. They were each married in the temple for more than nineteen years.

During and following a divorce it may be difficult for some grieving family members to attend church meetings.

"Today it was hard to be at church.....They showed part of a video about "Families are Forever". It's awful for a divorced person to realize that they no longer have a complete family. I feel it sometimes pulls people away from the church ... I need to remember to follow Christ and believe Christ. He has promised that if I do what is right I will have all that he has. That means a "forever family." Later: "When I look through my journal now, it upsets me. I see how I was so consumed with justification that I couldn't enjoy life ...I was trying to do my best and I didn't feel it was good enough. My spouse said that one of the reasons he left was because I made him feel guilty. I told him I didn't mean to 'guilt' him, and that I would go to counseling and learn how to improve communication, etc. 'No,' he said, his mind was made up. This made me carry more guilt. One thing I would say to a person going through divorce, 'Get rid of guilt, it doesn't do any good. Guilt gets you no where.'

Part of the guilt this sister was experiencing was "false guilt"; feeling guilty for events that are outside of our personal agency, responsibility, and control (see p. 78). True guilt for willful wrong-doing, in contrast, will lead us to repentance and personal growth as we change our sinful behavior.

"I called my sister today. She is in the depths of despair. She just finished her first week of full-time employment since her husband left about a month ago. She was physically and emotionally exhausted, and depressed. It was Easter Sunday and she had watched General Conference. She tried to find comfort in the Atonement and the words spoken. She desperately wants to keep her husband, temple marriage and children together. She ask me why Alma's father's prayer was answered by an angel appearing and convincing his son and Mosiah's sons to repent. Why didn't the same angel convince her husband to repent and stay with his family? She asks, 'Why do some people receive a miracle, while others do not?' She is a worthy member, with faith as strong as any I've known. She was so sad and depressed. She thought of asking her kindergartner to come and kneel by her bed and pray for her as she lay sobbing. She wondered if maybe the faith of a child's prayer would relieve her agony. I thought of the savior who felt the pain of the world's sins in Gethsemane. Please let this cup pass.

She also said she was hoping for a car accident to remove this pain and the future without her eternal companion. I cried with her, realizing her pain was beyond my comprehension. Will a new mate be provided? When and how? Could she and the kids love him as much as their biological father? So much faith is required."

A child writes about her plea to God:

"I remember getting down on my knees and asking my Father in Heaven to please help my parents to not get a divorce. When I received no answer, I felt all alone, like I wasn't getting any help for the pain I felt. It hurt for a very long time. I don't think I ever got over not getting my answer (spiritual injury). With time I accepted that my parents were going to get a divorce."

"My dad was excommunicated before my parent's divorce. It was embarrassing to have friends over, so I didn't do that much (My mom showed her anger even in front of my friends). I turned to my peers, especially boyfriends."

MARITAL DISCORD

Some couples experience a major loss in their marriage relationships without divorce. They stay in their marriages as they struggle to work out their problems and differences.

"My husband got involved with another woman. It has hurt me beyond words. We are trying to save our temple marriage. He is repenting and still attends church. However, I fear I don't trust him. I wonder who he is thinking about. Does he really love me? Will he stay? Can I forgive?"

"It's very hard to live with secrets. Everyone thinks I have the perfect spouse and marriage. I knew my spouse was curious about nudity and pornography before we were married. I assumed getting married would satisfy all curiosity and sexual desires. Now not only do I feel threatened (my body image), but I feel hurt that my spouse is breaking a commandment and threatening our eternal life together. I don't think my spouse really views it as a sin, which complicates our communication." (For marriage helps see Ch. 11.)

RAISING DIFFICULT CHILDREN IN DIFFICULT TIMES

Many of us have not considered that raising a difficult child could be a major loss for a parent. However, parenting is one of the toughest callings we may ever face. Most of us have little preparation, and soon learn child-rearing can be difficult even under ideal situations. For those who have difficult or rebellious children, the challenge can be enormous.

"On my daughter's sixteenth birthday she asked for a leather-bound standard works for her mission-preparation class, and a CTR ring in gold. She was a 4.0 honor student attending seminary daily. Five months later she ran away from home with a boy in the band at her school. His family hid her for three months until the boy broke up with her. She was sent back to us a different girl. She broke our hearts. She lasted at home for a couple of months. The drugs, alcohol, sex, and party life had changed her. The anti-church environment and anti-Mormon doctrine turned her into a purple, frizzy-haired modern hippie."

"I have a child with ADHD (Attention Deficit

Hyperactivity Disorder). No one seems to understand how difficult it is to cope. I feel judged by his behavior; wondering if others think that I'm not a good parent. It is so draining. When my husband comes home at night he tells me that I look so exhausted. I feel others think I am a bad mother because of his behavior. No one seems to understand that we are trying our best to help him. Many members give me advice about how to discipline him etc.. Teachers call, frustrated with him in classes at school and church. I didn't know having children could be so difficult and disappointing. I just don't know if I can cope. I don't see him ever being on his own."

"My son is nineteen years old. He has been addicted to drugs since he was about fifteen. It started with alcohol, combined with his low self-esteem and depression. We have tried to get him help many times without much success. He has tried counseling and medication. He struggled to graduate from high school and has lost many jobs. He has not attended church, nor been morally clean. I worry so much about him. I don't know how to help him. I've cried, prayed, fasted, and put his name on the temple prayer roll. My heart hurts so much as I watch him fail time and time again."

"I suspected our son was involved with alcohol and smoking. We discussed it with him often; however, he didn't seem to change. Unfortunately, it led to worse things. His grades dropped, he lost his job, and pulled further away from family support. The saddest part was when he came to us confessing he had sex with a girl while he was drunk. He hardly knows this girl!"

"My nineteen year old has dated the same girl since he was seventeen They are together almost every day. I am so nervous about all this close contact and time together. What if it results in an unwed pregnancy and he loses his opportunity to serve a mission or attend BYU?"

Many members of the Church have had their hearts broken and mourn the loss of their children not living the commandments, serving, praying, reading the scriptures or attending church. The scriptures promise that:
"Those that mourn will be sanctified and have eternal life." (Moses 7:45)

The following illustrates how most young parents start out with idealistic dreams concerning raising their children:
"My friend and I wanted children more than anything else in the world. We envisioned ourselves teaching them sweet Primary songs all day long; and that they would sit in awe at our feet as we shared our testimonies with them. Some of our children did respond to the Spirit. However, each of us had a rebellious teenager. It was confusing for us to understand how one child in our family could be so sensitive to the spirit, and another could be so unfeeling and rebellious. This lack of Spirit in our rebellious children has been a tremendous loss for both of us."

It is tragic to see how one child can break the tender hearts of their parents and wrack the spiritual climate in a home. Shattered expectations that we have for our children may develop into a significant loss and require grief processing.

(For specific help and more information on difficult children see chapter 12.)

UNWED PARENTS

Each year more than a million unwed pregnancies occur in Canada and the United States. Approximately fifteen thousand of those pregnancies involve LDS birth mothers, which averages about one birth mother per ward per year. Most of those who keep and single-parent their infants will never marry in the temple. Those who place the child with faithful adoptive couples are much more likely to eventually marry in the temple themselves. Seventy percent of the single parents in America will need welfare assistance. Whether the birth parent single-parents, marries or places the infant for adoption, it becomes a stressful series of losses and disappointments for everyone concerned and involved.

"I never heard 'I love you's' at home, so I guess I craved to hear and feel love. I dressed in a way to get attention and it became a power. I liked it and wanted and needed more. I made many mistakes."

"I got drunk with a friend one night. After, we went to visit some girls and one of them was very aggressive and knew what she was doing. The alcohol seemed to soften my previous resistive powers. I lost my virginity. Now she thinks she is pregnant!"

An unwed mother writes after placing her baby for adoption, marrying and having another child:
"It is always so ironic how tragedy can bring a family together. I had been battling endometriosis before I got pregnant with my only child. I have now had a full hysterectomy including my ovaries. Needless to say, my emotions have been a roller coaster. I am on hormones plus I am still dealing with

the fact that I am no longer able to have babies. I never dreamed that I would be faced with this. I am learning 'never say never'. Who would have ever thought that a young teenager placing her baby for adoption would come full circle to this. The worst part of it is listening to my only daughter pray for a brother or sister. She keeps telling me that her brothers and sisters are waiting in heaven for her to bring them home. What do I say? It is so overwhelming. When I placed my baby for adoption, all I could think about was how much better he would be without me for a mom. I get so depressed when I think of where all this has come to."

"As hard as it seems for me and my mother to give my baby to someone else, we want him to be sealed to a father and a mother in the temple."

"Once I became pregnant I knew I had to become active in the church, even if I had to go by myself. I knew I was responsible for my baby and I took that responsibility very deeply. I remember sitting in meetings while taking care of my baby and feeling so alone. I felt that everyone else had this perfect happy home with a priesthood holder and sealed in the temple. I didn't have this."

"Both my daughter and I had a powerful spiritual confirmation that the baby she was carrying should be placed with a mother and father who could be sealed to him in the temple. The peace that we both felt is what helped me let go of my grandchild and avoid additional feelings of pain and grief."

LDS Family Services offers free counseling, support and adoption-planning for unwed parents.

CHAPTER 4

MEMBERS DISCUSS THEIR LOSS FOLLOWING ABUSE, SAME-GENDER ATTRACTION, LIVING SINGLE, EMPTY NEST AND MIDLIFE CRISIS, HOMELESSNESS, AND UNEMPLOYMENT.

ABUSE

In 1997, three million claims of child abuse and neglect were reported in the U.S.; 963,870 were confirmed. (7 4/12/99 p. 32) In 1999 there were approximately nine hundred thousand confirmed reports of child abuse. (8 4/2/99) Fortunately the statistics have dropped for the fourth year in a row. Nevertheless, abuse is a serious concern in and out of the church:

"We warn that individuals...who abuse spouse and offspring,...will one day stand accountable before God." (1)

Abuse comes in many forms: physical, spiritual, emotional, economical and sexual. Abuse may be intense and obvious, or more subtle. Someone may call us names, put us down, push, shove or physically restrain us. They may want to control where we go, what we think, or to whom we talk to. We may receive intimidating looks, gestures or threats causing us fear, guilt and shame. (2 3/99)

Many women who could and should get out of abusive situations don't.

"I had begged my daughter to get out of her physically abusive relationship. It ultimately cost her her life. I am the one who found her a couple of days later in her apartment. I am in total agony recovering from the death of my beautiful young daughter."

An estimated 1.9 million women are physically assaulted every year in the U.S. Sadly, it is most often by an intimate partner. (2 3/99)

"I was shocked when after a few weeks of marriage my husband physically abused me. It scared me, and I wondered how I could ever get a temple divorce."

The scriptures remind us:
"We have learned by sad experience that it is the nature and disposition of almost all men, as soon as they get a little authority, as they suppose, they will immediately begin to exercise unrighteous dominion." (D&C 121:39)

"I grew up with a verbally abusive father. I especially disliked hearing him yell at my mother. I often heard him force her to have sex. He was very active in the church and would often apologize in a general way for his bad behavior. However, damage was still done. Now I overreact to my husband, if he even slightly raises his voice. Also, I always want to be in control, no one can ever take advantage of me...even when they aren't trying! After my father's death, my mother would express guilt for some of the relief she felt having him gone. She said she liked living alone and had no desire to remarry, and was happier than she had ever been."

In Jacob 2:31-35 we read about the sorrow and mourning of wives and daughters who were abused by husbands and fathers.

"And I will not suffer...that the cries of the fair daughters...shall come up...because of the wickedness and abominations of their husbands...I will visit them with a sore curse...ye have broken the hearts of your tender wives, and lost the confidence of your children."

The following quote is from a young girl who was abused many times in her life and shared the abusive experiences with someone close to her. The following is what she wrote in a letter:

"Do you think differently of me now? Please don't. I already feel different. Like when my ward went to do baptisms, I did dress out and everything, but when they called me to the font I didn't feel like my body was pure enough to do the baptisms for these people. I felt really bad inside and it hurt inside to think that my body wasn't clean enough to do it. I stopped saying my prayers for a long time, but just a few days ago I started saying them again and boy did I feel good. I hope I have enough faith in myself that I can do these baptisms."

Then she wrote the following poem:

I said a prayer for you today
And I know God must have heard
I felt the answer in my heart
Although he spoke no word.
I asked that He'd be near to you
At the start of each new day
To grant you health and blessings

and a friend to share your way.
I asked for happiness for you
In all things great and small
BUT IT WAS FOR HIS LOVING CARE
I PRAYED FOR MOST OF ALL.

How many prayers will an abused child offer, exercising faith that God will stop the abuse they are enduring; believing that God can and will intervene in their lives? As the abuse continues, in spite of their faith and prayers, they experience confusion and begin to question their worth. This challenge is further complicated for some when they finally seek help from family and church leaders only to have their claims denied by the perpetrator and not believed by those whose help and support they desperately need.

"My mother got angry with me when I told her about my sexual abuse. She said, "He (brother) would never do that!" Consequently, I couldn't get help until I was an adult."

There are many secondary losses associated with abuse. Loss of self-esteem, poor body image, eating disorders, sexual problems, nightmares, troubled relationships, excessive need to be in control, addictions, physical and emotional illness, etc.

"Many men and women have gone out of this life...without their vile crimes detected. They may have served in church callings; had wonderful reputations, wealth, good health, and glowing funeral services. ...the demands of justice reach beyond the veil." (3 p.13)

A mother struggling with the principle of moral agency writes:

"I struggle with the suffering of little innocent children. How people can hurt them physically, emotionally or sexually is hard for me to understand. How does God know of these injustices and not intervene?"

"I sensed as a young child it was wrong. However, I loved the attention, friendship, and relationship time my abuser offered me. When I became a teenager the sexual gratification became part of it. I knew it was wrong then, it was just hard to break away."

"I'm not sure how old I was. I was wearing a dress, sitting on his lap and I felt his hand on my underwear. I was so uncomfortable and afraid, I froze, not knowing what to do!"

Most young children love their parents unconditionally. They hug and kiss them even if they are homely, wrinkled, and have bad breath! Abused children often defend their parents or others who have abused them. This is one reason children have a difficult time getting out of an abusive situation. Another obvious reason is because they are only children, with minimal control over their circumstances.

"My father died before I was old enough to confront him with the sexual abuse he had inflicted upon me."

The following quote has been a comfort for many who have felt the results of abuse.

"When the future conduct of a violated one is warped and veers away from normal Christian conduct due to early abuse, the Lord will be extremely merciful to those thus forced and violated. It is my belief that the Lord will judge them for what they would have been had the abuse never occurred." (3 p.12)

"The sexual abuse that my husband endured as a young child led to his homosexuality, which ultimately led to our divorce."

SAME-GENDER ATTRACTION

It is estimated that two million marriages include a homosexual spouse. A number of these couples are LDS. Some same-gender-attracted individuals live alone, never marrying or practicing their homosexuality.

Some same-gender individuals marry in the temple and choose to live heterosexual lives, bearing and parenting children. Many have testimonies of the restored gospel and desire desperately to change. Many are sitting in sacrament meetings around the world, holding and loving their children, yet feeling hurt and lonely because they believe few can or will ever understand their anger, grief, pain and confusion.

"I was sexually abused as a child. I remember thinking when I was to be ordained a deacon that I could become 'clean'. I talked about it with my bishop, seeking a worthy feeling. I was active in the church and fulfilled my priesthood responsibilities. I served an honorable mission. Although I struggled with masturbation at times, I was determined to overcome my problem. I married a wonderful, spiritual woman in the LDS temple. We have several children. I have undergone years of therapy through LDS Family Services. I had many counseling hours with bishops and stake presidents. However, after children and many years of marriage we are divorcing because of my homosexuality. Now, I wonder if I didn't pray hard enough. I wonder if I didn't study enough. I wonder if I gave up. Did I give it my all?"

"I thought my husband would be able to overcome his homosexuality. He served a mission and married me in the temple. I love him and want him forever. However, we have decided on divorce because he cannot function in the marriage. He is not sexually attracted to me. It is very painful to suffer such an eternal loss. I sometimes feel like a failure and don't want to give up. However, after all the prayers, blessings, fasting, and therapy, he hasn't changed. I think his death would be an easier solution. At least I would know I could have him in the eternities."

Some same-gender-attracted individuals receive healing or control over their struggles, others do not. It is a painful and disappointing challenge for them and their families.

"I have done everything—the counseling, bishop and stake president meetings, prayer, support groups, sports, reading, etc. The only hope I see at this point is a miracle. As I weigh things out in my mind, it seems only logical and right that we should get divorced for my wife's sake. However, there is a great deal to fear: the effect on our children, financial devastation, and loss of self-esteem. Could I handle losing my family eternally? On the other hand, I would feel some relief, a decision would be made and I would be able to stop feeling like I have to pretend and cover up my real feelings. What do I do?!"

President Gordon B. Hinckley offers compassion and important counsel:

"Our hearts reach out to those who refer to themselves as gays and lesbians. We love and honor them as sons and daughters of God. They are welcome in the Church. It is expected, however, that they follow the same God-given rules of sexual conduct that apply to everyone....The Church's opposition to attempts to legalize same-gender marriage should never be interpreted as justification for hatred, intolerance or abuse of those who profess homosexual tendencies." (4 10/9/99, p.17)

The loss and grief issues emerging from homosexual lifestyles are significant, not only for the same-gender-attracted individual, but also for the many family members and friends who are left wondering why their circumstances are not different.

"I'm honestly happier than I've ever been. I'm leaving my worldly value system and becoming a spiritually-oriented person in Christ. Everyone needs to do this, whether they have homosexual feelings or not. We just need to have faith. If Jesus was able to heal the sick and raise the dead, certainly he can heal my homosexual problems." (9 p.243)

LIVING SINGLE/ NEVER A PARENT/ NEVER MARRIED

There are single adults in the Church who will never marry or become parents in this life. Some are quick to remind singles that theirs is not an "eternal loss." They are reminded that they will receive these blessings in the next life. However, do we allow them to mourn and grieve for the loss that they are experiencing and the life experiences that they are currently missing? Do we friendship and welcome them at church and invite them to church activities? Do we encourage them to serve and find meaning in life without the responsibility and blessings of a spouse or children?

"Sometimes it is very painful to watch my younger

brothers and sisters marry and have children. I try to support them and their families. My patriarchal blessing promised that I would marry and have children. Now I am more than fifty years old. Going through menopause is especially difficult."

Some single members would like to experience parenthood. Single individuals can adopt children in many states and from some foreign countries where children do not have biological parents. LDS Family Services and Church leaders counsel that whenever possible a baby should have both a father and a mother, and be sealed to those parents in the temple.

"I've been single for all of my forty six years and a member of the church for twenty one years. My experience has been that many members who are single have feelings of inadequacy and being left out. It has helped me to accept callings, attend church activities, and reach out to others." (4 E.K. Young 1-9-99, p.15)

"I have learned over the years that if I wish to be included in someone else's circle, I need to include him or her in mine." (4 M.Banac, 1-9-99, p.15)

"My biggest problem is I get lonely, not lonely in the sense that I can have lots of people around, but lonely for a close, intimate, eternal relationship."

"I sit in the very back during church. I feel a little uncomfortable because the church is made up mostly of intact families. I feel somewhat judged because it's been several years and I haven't found someone to marry."

FULL/EMPTY NEST SYNDROME

The Church emphasizes the importance of families. "Mothers are primarily responsible for the nurture of their children". Fathers are primarily responsible to preside, protect and provide the necessities of life. (1) Many parents put their children's needs above their own as they sacrifice over many years, raising and training them. I remember feeling overwhelmed with motherhood and my "full nest" when we had five young children at home. One child was in a wheelchair, another had ADD, and the youngest was still a nursing newborn. Dennis was often gone, working hard at his career as well as being a busy bishop. Looking back, I am amazed that my "full nest" brought such stress, adversity and feelings of loss. Ironically, later I would experience similar feelings when the nest started to empty.

Life starts to change as our children grow up, go off to college, serve missions and marry. Many women (and some men) in the church develop what some call the "Empty Nest Syndrome". The loss of children living at home often results in mourning and grief.

"When my first child went into the mission field, I felt a sadness that is hard to describe. My youngest child started school and I am alone most of the day. I also have a teenager who is rarely home and not interested in doing family things. I thought I couldn't wait until I had this free time; however, I feel empty and lonely."

"When my first son graduated from high school and left for his mission, I was told it would be hard to watch him go knowing that he was all grown up and may never live at home again. However, I was so proud that he had decided to go on a mission, that I was thrilled. The farewell was a big high for me. However, a few weeks after he left, I fell into a depression of sorts."

A non-LDS psychologist near our home in Texas was confused when he saw LDS women in his practice struggle as their children grew up and left home. He observed significant grief as these mothers attempted to adjust to their children leaving the nest.

His confusion resulted from his observation that non-LDS parents have—on the average—one or two children, and when they are finally grown, celebrate recovering the time and privacy they have missed.

How individuals are raised including their beliefs and life expectations will all affect whether or not they experience the "Empty Nest Syndrome."

For example, even though I went to college, earned a degree and qualified myself for a career, what mattered most to me was becoming a mother. When my children started growing up and leaving, I felt sadness. It took time for me to redefine my identity, purpose and roles.

A friend of ours and mother of six grown children said:
"Some children are harder to let go than others."

Confirming this, another mother said:
"When one of my children moved away, I cried and cried. When another one went, I was thrilled! A burden was lifted."

MIDLIFE CRISIS

Midlife is defined as the middle years of our life. It is usually between the ages of thirty and fifty. A midlife crisis may occur because of the struggles we often go through. Midlife is a time of reflection. We may discover during midlife that certain long-held assumptions and beliefs about ourselves and our world are not true. We may find that all the hopes and dreams we have worked and sacrificed for will not be realized. We might race toward personal goals only to be dissatisfied when we finally reach them. Some of our wants and aspirations have been artificially created and prove to be illusionary and empty in the end.

"When my husband turned forty, he started to grow a mustache and beard. He bought some 'mod' clothes and a new car. It wasn't long before he left me for someone else. Of course, he also became inactive."

"My ex-husband is homosexual. He served a mission and married me in the temple. He received counseling over the years and did not practice his homosexuality until he turned forty and had a mid-life crisis! Then he was excommunicated and we divorced."

"I had no idea a mid-life crisis would feel like this. I thought mine would be dieting, buying new clothes, and wanting to flirt. Here I am, just lost, not knowing where to go. The first half of my life seemed all planned out. Now, what about the second half? In what direction do I go?"

Midlife brings a variety of experiences to Church members. Often they are surprised and confused by their feelings.

"I always assumed mid-life crisis meant I would want to have a face-lift or something similar. However, my crisis came after I got overly stressed and decided I needed to cut back on the many things I was doing in my life. At the same time I was released from a busy calling at church. I found myself alone while the kids were in school, thinking, "Okay, what do I do now?" Should I read the scriptures, clean the house, start the wash, work in the yard, plan dinner or family night? (These things were usually somehow done between my volunteer work, outside commitments and church callings) Somehow, it didn't seem as exciting to face all these chores day after day. Why wasn't I adjusting to all this down time? I decided to add an institute class to my agenda which would help me with my scripture study and get me out of the house occasionally. But every day I prayed, Lord, please help me be content. I don't want to get myself all busy and stressed again. This is what I've always wanted and waited for, isn't it? Think of all the things I can do now with this extra time. I kept thinking, 'what now, what next, what direction'? This was my mid-life crisis."

"When I would go for my chemotherapy and radiation treatments, most of the people there were a lot older than I. I found that we had a lot in common because of our cancers. I soon felt that I was learning what it is like to grow old, get sick and die. I think I experienced a midlife crisis. The chemotherapy and radiation also put me into menopause early."

"Many of the assumptions, dreams, and hopes I had when I first married have faded: The number of children I wanted, where I wished to live, my health, how I thought God would bless and protect me, how righteous my husband and children would be, how church leadership would work. I am trying to adjust to reality and redefine those assumptions, hopes and dreams. I am trying not to dwell on what cannot be. It has left me with a sadness that is sometimes frightening."

As we grow from childhood to adulthood, we experience many changes and adjustments. Our days of innocence and make-believe are generally over. It is not that we don't want to believe and dream, but too much has happened and we begin to focus more on reality. This is part of growing and learning. This reality often hits us square in the face at midlife.

Oftentimes we are not only confronted with our own problems, but also our children's and even grandchildren's challenges!

"My grandparents were shaken by my parents' divorce. My parents are disappointed their daughters are childless."

Some of us in a mid-life situation attempt to hold on to those things that by nature, circumstance or choice are no longer within our reach. "No matter how hard you squeeze a handful of sand, you will never get oil out of it." (Tibetan saying) We also may realize that all the sorrow we have been through from grasping at the unreachable was not necessary or even helpful. This painful realization is part of the process of "letting go" and redefining our circumstances.

LOSS OF HOME/MOVING/MISSIONARY SERVICE

Many years ago we lost the top floor of our home to a fire. I was surprised how difficult it was to cope. We moved into the basement for three months. The electricity was out for a while.

I remember bathing our three small children in a shower with no lights and no hot water (I went to a hotel later that day!). I wondered how others dealt with losing all their possessions as well as their home. We gained insight, in a small way, to the impact of natural disasters. Research shows that depression increases with natural disasters. Depression elevates by thirty to sixty percent for those who have experienced earthquakes, hurricanes, and tornadoes. It increases by fourteen percent with floods. (5 5/4/99)

Dennis and I feel deeply for those who have been displaced or lost their homes from the ravages of nature or war. Many victims and refugees have suffered multiple losses; not only experiencing the loss of home and possessions, but also having to endure or witness rape, murder, and torture.

Dennis was sent by LDS Charities and LDS Family Services to provide assistance and evaluate the needs of host families caring for Kosovo refugees and the full-time missionaries serving in Albania during the 1999 NATO bombing. As he met with refugees and heard their terrible stories of abuse and suffering, he was overwhelmed at their loss and grief. How could human beings lose so much and survive emotionally? Dennis asked a young man in Albania, a social worker from Kosovo, "Why do you want to go back when your homes are destroyed?" He answered, "Our land is still there, and our hope is not destroyed." He also recounted horror stories of torture, murder, rape and other atrocities. Those who cause such suffering may face the fate described by Mormon to his son Moroni: "How can we expect that God will stay his hand...?" (Moroni 9: 7-21) The loss-grief recovery process will be long and hard for many war refugees. Their grief may be complicated because someone purposely chose to cause their suffering. The term *Traumatic Loss* includes victims of: crime, natural disasters, abuse of power, violations of human rights, health challenges, homicidal deaths, and forced displacement.

Growing up and leaving home for some can constitute a major life adjustment, producing feelings of loss and grief.

"I miss living near my family and friends. My husband says our ward should become our family and should be enough support. I do pretty well most of the time; however, other times I resent that I have had to follow my husband's work and live far from my home and relatives."

"I grew up and lived in the same town for many years after my marriage. I was surrounded by family and friends. My firstborn was doted on, and we were always busy with family home evenings and get-togethers.

Then my husband took a job about one thousand miles away. After we moved and settled, I was home alone. The days were long and I had no friends or family. The area looked and felt so foreign. Although still in the U.S., I felt like I was in another country! I cried a lot and was so homesick. Thank goodness for the church. Although it took a long time, I made new friends. My sadness and depression softened, but it was just never quite like home."

Often we underestimate the affects of moving on ourselves and our children. I moved eighteen times before I was six years old, due to my father's work and education. My mother worked part-time while Dad was getting his Ph.D. I remember feeling sad when I had to say goodbye to friends and had to adjust to a new house, school and friends. I often wondered if that is why, at nine years old, I started suffering from "separation anxiety". Now as an adult, whenever we move or I experience serious change or loss I revert back to those anxious feelings I felt as a child.

We recognize the good of missionary work, for the missionaries as well as the individuals they teach. We teach that if they "lose themselves in service to the Lord, they will truly find themselves". (Mark 8:35-6; Luke 9:24-5) When missionaries return home they share their increased testimonies and recount wonderful experiences with their ward. However, many members are not familiar with how painful their adjustments can be as each missionary sheds the "natural man" and finds his or her new self in the Lord. The movie *God's Army* depicts this transformation well.

A missionary writes after arriving in his first area:
"Reality has hit! Not a familiar face in sight. I've had better nights, trying to collect my thoughts and fall asleep on uncomfortable beds with elders snoring. I'm way out of my comfort zone. I feel like I'm losing my personality. I'm not sure I want my kids to go through this. I don't feel like the same person at all, like I never existed before the mission." Signed "Love, Elder I don't know any more."

This loss of self identity is common to many types of loss. A new elder in the field said:
"My uncomfortable moments still seem to outlast the good ones. I get troubled and hate feeling this way. I'm not sure what it is that's bothering me (confused by his grief). I try not to think too much because then I get stressed out (denies his grief) I've developed a lot of ways to deal with things (coping mechanisms). It's overwhelming."

"While reading out loud to my companion through all the rules and things I had to learn in my binder, I stopped as I felt overwhelmed and tears started hitting the pages. It reminded me of pre-school when I couldn't cut on the lines and tears fell on my work. However, Mom came and rescued me then! Mom, where are you now?"

"Today was my first day in the field. Before I knew it I had borrowed a bike, and was peddling as fast as I could, wearing my suit and a helmet and couldn't keep up with my comp! I was sweating, tore my pants, and felt tired, scared and overwhelmed."

"I've wrecked on my bike, froze at doorsteps, and had my helmet spit in. However, I have had feelings come over me that I would not trade for the world."

Unfortunately some missionaries cannot endure all of this change, loss and grief. Some will need professional help to resolve their serious mental and emotional struggles. If they have to come home early, they add feelings of guilt and failure to their pain. The grief-recovery process for these young men and women can leave permanent scars. Fortunately, with sufficient faith and help from the Lord, most missionaries work through their loss and grief issues and learn to love the work, the people they serve and adjust to their new lives as ambassadors of the Lord.

LOSS OF FINANCES OR EMPLOYMENT

Financial reversals, unemployment, and underemployment constitute major losses for many. They are usually followed by additional or secondary losses, such as loss of self-esteem or identity. Many times marriage and family relationships also suffer.

Years ago President Hinckley said:

"A man out of work is of special moment to the church because, deprived of his inheritance, he is on trial as Job was on trial—for his integrity. As days lengthen into weeks and months and even years of adversity. The hurt grows deeper, and he is sorely tempted to 'curse God and die.' Continued economic dependence breaks him, it humiliates him if he is strong, spoils him if he is weak. Sensitive or calloused, despondent or indifferent, rebellious or resigned—either way, he is threatened with spiritual ruin, for the dole is the seedbed of discontent, wrong thinking, alien beliefs. The church cannot hope to save a man on Sunday if during the week it is a complacent witness to the crucifixion of his soul." (6)

"Logically I suspected I could lose my job or financial security someday. It happens to lots of people. However, when it did happen, emotionally I was very sick, scared, and upset. I wondered what else would go wrong in my life. I felt vulnerable, that things weren't within my control."

"My father still feels shame for not providing well for us over the years. Now as an adult I see the scars left from years of struggling so."

"In a very short time our family experienced an unwed pregnancy, a diagnosis of a possible terminal illness, and I lost my employment. I think worrying about whether I can support my family now is more than I can bear."

"We had a secure family and good marriage until my husband lost his position at work. It damaged his self-esteem and changed our relationship, family and marriage. He was humiliated, irritable, depressed and angry for years. He died an early death and I 'm not sure he ever fully recovered from that experience."

"Due to my divorce I have lost my financial security. I am living on less than half of what I was used to before the divorce. We have had to move out of our home and live in a small apartment. I cannot even treat my children to McDonalds or buy them clothes. I try to be thankful for what I do have because there are so many in the world with much less. It is just such an adjustment for me and the children."

"My husband seems so preoccupied with our finances. He is always trying to find new ways to increase our income and decrease our outflow of money. I understand that this is his primary role and responsibility; however, I resent his encouraging me to work more outside the home. I wish money wasn't so important to him and that he could put his concerns to more of our spiritual needs."

Grief can become complicated when members cannot find work because they have been taught and believe in the eternal significance of work. "In the sweat of thy face thou shalt eat bread." (Genesis 3:19)

Within a marriage, it is primarily a man's responsibility to provide and protect. (1) If he is unable to preform his role, it may create feelings of anger, guilt, failure, and helplessness.

SECTION II

LOSS SYMPTOMS AND TOOLS
FOR HEALING

Most individuals dealing with loss will experience symptoms in each of the following five areas or dimensions; Spiritual, Physical, Social, Emotional and Intellectual. Each dimension influences all other areas, while at the same time being influenced by each of the other dimensions. (See figure #3) Following each dimension's symptoms, we will attempt to provide suggestions and interventions for healing.

CHAPTER 5

EMOTIONAL SYMPTOMS RESULTING FROM LOSS AND TOOLS FOR HEALING

One of life's most meaningful emotions, happiness, can be compromised by weighty adversity and loss. The word bereaved means "to rob." Those in mourning are often "robbed" of something or someone that was very significant to them.

Acute grief is often experienced when we are facing a serious crisis or enduring a significant loss. Symptoms of acute grief include disbelief, denial, shock and numbness.

SHOCK, NUMBNESS AND DISBELIEF

"How can this be? I can't believe it!"

Loss often changes how and what we expected our life to be. Our assumptive world has been altered or violated. Dennis and I had personally never felt such deep pain until Cameron died. We, like many, felt, "This is not fair!" and asked, "Why us?" We were in a state of confusion. The disbelief, sadness, loneliness, fear, regret, and despair initially seemed to overpower us. It became difficult to fully experience happiness, joy, love, or spirituality for some time. At times it became difficult to concentrate on even simple tasks. Our normal coping behaviors had been depleted for the first time in our lives.

DENIAL

For some the disbelief and denial may remain for weeks, months, or even years. Sometimes friends and relatives contribute to this denial. They may think or say things like, "I won't talk about it if you don't." (1) Some of us go a step beyond denial in our attempt to cope. This is called *repression*: an unconscious forgetting of the traumatic event. We stuff the loss far from our conscious memory. Unfortunately, emotions not dealt with on a conscious level may appear later as physical or mental illness, generalized anxiety, panic attacks, or post-traumatic stress syndrome.

Some of us use avoidance patterns to deny our grief. These are behaviors and attitudes that help us delay feeling pain. Avoidance patterns include purposely postponing, displacing, or minimizing the emotions or event. Some individuals become obsessed with shopping, working, eating, intellectualizing, traveling, exercising, crusading, or drugging their pain.

There may be secondary losses resulting from changes and adjustments that might be denied initially. The divorcee who tries to maintain the same financial status finally realizes that she must sell her home to survive financially. Another may have to return to work to support her family. It will often take doses of reality and painful experiences for us to totally realize all we must face in the future. However, with patience, time, and grief work, our denial can subside and eventually most will be able to successfully face the hurtful realities of our new life.

"I had no idea there would be so many other changes and adjustments following my loss. If I'd had to face all my losses at once I would never make it. Step by step, I am slowly adjusting."

DEPRESSION

A psychologist counseled one of his depressed clients to go to the circus to lift his sadness. He thought seeing and laughing at the cheerful clown could relieve his client's depression. The client responded, "I am the circus clown!" How many of us have to wear a mask and play the clown because of our depression or because others fail to recognize our pain?

"I feel like I'm in a big black hole. Nothing feels or looks good to me. I'm afraid I can't keep going."

Situational depression can be a reaction to a traumatic event and a component of grief. It can be a result of the sadness and deep sorrow we have experienced. Depression can influence our thoughts, moods, and behaviors. When events seem beyond our control, the helplessness that follows often leads to depression. We may feel worried, overwhelmed, and anxious. Intense anxiety can also lead to depression. We may feel agitated, tense and lack the ability to concentrate or even remember what we were going to do. We may feel empty, fearful, helpless, hopeless, worthless, and abandoned. We may physically move slowly and feel emotionally dead inside. Depression can also result when our anger is turned inward. When we blame ourselves, talk or think negative thoughts about ourselves, or keep all our feelings bottled up inside, we may find ourselves in a deep black hole of depression.

Every year more than eleven million Americans suffer from a serious depression. Depression is often brought on by loss. Job lost all he owned, in addition to his loved ones. He also suffered physical pain and experienced intense emotions, including depression: "My soul is weary." (Job 10:1)

One woman said, "I've lost my song." Another said, "The worst thing in life is to be alive...but dead inside."

Some depressive symptoms can bring changes in our body's ability to function. We may experience changes in weight, sleep, and appetite. We might not be able to perform as well at home, school or at work. We may not be able to interact with others with the same confidence. If our situational depression persists it can develop into a clinical depression, qualifying in certain instances for the diagnosis of major depressive disorder. (2)

A *clinical* depression not only changes our ability to function but can lead to a total inability to function. In extreme cases, individuals become incapacitated and are unable to care for themselves and lose their desire to live. Fortunately, even serious depression can be successfully treated. Clinical depression, however, does not usually respond to the basic self-help tools alone (exercise, sunlight, diet, writing therapy, etc.). It may require professional intervention, psychotherapy and/or medication.

Depression can often lead to suicide if left untreated. (See p. 22)

ANXIETY

Anxiety is a common symptom of adversity. Anxious feelings usually come when someone or something we value is being threatened? It could include the threat of losing love, security, esteem, integrity, control, success, etc.

"The other night the storm picked up so violently. I panicked and ran to find my three-year-old son. He is my only child. I have had three miscarriages and lost both of my tubes. I cannot bear another loss. I am angry I have these fears."

Job describes his anxiety as he faced his multiple sufferings and losses:

"For the thing which I greatly feared is come upon me, and that which I was afraid of is come unto me. I was not in safety, neither had I rest, neither was I quiet; yet trouble came." (Job 3:25-26)

Our anxiety may appear in a variety of behaviors. After Cameron died I dove into overactivity. It may have been an attempt to validate my worth or redefine my purpose, now that I no longer had Cameron to care for. I used my busyness in doing tasks in an attempt to find relief from my grief. Through my overactivity I was determined to make my life significant, meaningful, and productive in spite of my pain. All of this overactivity helped me cope as best I could; however, eventually I had to slow down to prevent exhaustion.

If we stay in this "overactive" or "avoidance" mode for long periods of time, we may become stuck in the grief process, unable to totally resolve important issues because we are too busy. Some research shows that overdoing or overactivity actually increases our anxiety and stress. We need to avoid taking on more responsibility than we can realistically handle. Even small challenges can seem more stressful during the loss and grief process.

There are, in addition, many physical symptoms that can accompany anxiety. "My pulse raced, I couldn't breathe, sit still, or concentrate. I went into over-activity, trying to do a hundred things at once. I got a lot of things done, but my anxiety never left me."

(The self-help tools listed later in this chapter offer ideas for dealing with anxiety; however, if anxiety turns into panic attacks, professional help and medication may be needed.)

BARGAINING (3)

Bargaining is a step in the grieving process that commonly occurs during adversity. We may make promises to ourselves, others, or God. In return we seek acceptance, answers to our prayers, improved health, or some other miracle. This bargaining can go on for days, months or even years.

A man prayed:

I will live a better life and be kinder if you will please spare my wife's life.

ANGER

Anger is a common emotion with any loss and can indicate the beginning of healing and acceptance. Women (and female children) often turn their anger inward, displaying less physical aggression than men. Men (and male children) often manifest their anger openly. The consequences of grief, associated with a significant loss, may resemble rage in males. (16) Society seems to accept and expects men's outward display of anger and women's inward manifestations of grief through sadness and tears. This contributes to the reality that some women do not feel they can openly express their anger. Many women find ways to hold onto their anger. Unfortunately anger repressed, ignored, shelved or turned inward can lead to depression, confusion, and guilt.

It is common, though not excusable, for men to strike out at the very people they love most. They are often unsure where or how to productively direct their anger. It was helpful to me after Cameron died when Dennis said, "When I act or seem angry, it just means I'm feeling sad and hurt inside."

Anger can also hide other deep emotions. It can be an indication of unmet needs or expectations. Our assumptions of how our life should have been are often compromised. This secondary loss of a safe, predictable world complicates our grieving. We may now feel vulnerable and afraid of additional impending future losses.

Anger can be a sign of healing, so we shouldn't ignore it. Even if we feel anger towards relatives, medical staff, friends, or God, it is helpful to express our sometimes-conflicting emotions. For a time we may even feel life is meaningless. We might feel specific anger toward God for allowing our families to suffer. Even Job, whom God loved and accepted as right-eous, expressed anger toward God as he searched for meaning:

"Let the day perish wherein I was born...Why died I not from the womb?...Why is light given to a man whose hid, and whom God hath hedged in?" (Job 3:3-13)

"I cry unto thee, and thou dost not hear me: I stand up and thou regardest me not. Thou art become cruel to me..." (Job 30:20-21)

Following a crisis, anger directed towards deity, or church leaders representing God, is common among all religions. It may be more intense for faithful members who believed that God should have blessed them and prevented their tragedy. Most LDS members have been taught and believe that God is good and loves them. If we experience feelings of anger toward God it can produce intense guilt, complicating the grieving process. It is a frightening experience to face a serious loss if we feel like we are also losing our faith, support and comfort from God. (See spiritual tools in chapter 9.)

GUILT

Guilt is another emotion that is common with any traumatic event or serious loss. For many this is the most exhausting and difficult emotion to deal with.

"Guilt feelings are often a combination of many different feelings rather than one simple feeling...it's a messy mixture of insecurity, self-doubt, self-condemnation, self-judgment, anxiety, and fear."(4)

"If I had just noticed that something was wrong earlier and caught it sooner, I know I could have prevented this whole thing."

"I did so many things wrong. If I had just done things differently this wouldn't have happened."

As I work with families of the terminally ill, I am reminded of the intense guilt experienced during the illness and after the patient dies. The caregivers ask, "Did I do enough, was I kind enough, should I have kept them at home, or placed them for better care, what if...should I ...?" Those caring for the disabled express these same guilt-ridden phrases.

I wrote in my journal about my guilt, long after Cameron's death:

"I keep remembering how I got angry at him a few months before his death. What he did was really not his fault. I shamed him and made him cry. He went to school late with red eyes. Even though I apologized when he got home from school, it hasn't erased the guilty event from my memory."

74

Children may also experience guilt when dealing with loss: One child said, "If I hadn't wished my sister dead, she wouldn't be dying today." Another said, "If I had been a better boy, I wouldn't have gotten sick."

Guilt is a painful component of grief for many members of the church because we often feel we should have been able to control what has happened through our faith, prayers, or righteous living. "What did I do wrong? Am I responsible for this event?" The guilt-ridden words, I "should have", or "shouldn't have" may haunt us for a long time. It is an overwhelming burden for many to carry and endure.

Guilt was a strong emotion for both Dennis and I after Cam's death. We felt responsible for his safety and care. I wrote the following soon after Cameron's death:

"I was surprised by our doctor's advice. He informed me that Cameron's hips had deteriorated and he would need to have surgery within six months. Our appointment that day was for his scoliosis (a crooked spine) and for his back brace adjustments. The doctor had simply ordered the hip x-rays as a second thought. I could see tears swelling up in Cameron's big brown eyes . I tried to reassure him. I told him that during the surgery he would be asleep and it wouldn't hurt and that when he woke up he would get medication to keep him comfortable. I told him all the benefits of the surgery. The doctor had thought maybe his knee pain was coming from his partial hip dislocation. The surgery could possibly remove this pain so he could ride his adapted tricycle better. Cam was very trusting and obedient. He would do whatever we felt was best for him.

Because I was a concerned mother and pediatric nurse, I wanted to know all the details and names of all the procedures. I went home and researched the medical procedures that Cameron's doctors had recommended. I sought other professional's opinions. Dennis and Cameron trusted the doctor's and my decision that surgery was best. When it ultimately took his life, guilt haunted me for a long time."

Guilt resulting from failed attempts to protect those we love is portrayed well in the film *Robin Hood* starring Kevin Costner. Robin had made what he thought was the best decision to ensure protection of his beloved and trusted blind friend, Duncan. He sent him away from the fighting and danger...only to find that he had been ruthlessly murdered anyway! Robin felt enormous sorrow and guilt! Duncan was so perfect and obedient, Robin didn't feel he deserved to die. The guilt he felt for his decision was apparent. Then his partner, the great Azeem, seeing Robin's anguish, offered these words of counsel: "There are no perfect men, just perfect intentions."

Most of us also have "perfect intentions" concerning the well-being of our loved ones. Sometimes situations and events beyond our control go wrong. Even with the best plans and precautions, things go astray and accidents happen. Every day innocent children and adults become ill, injured or die in spite of our best efforts to protect them. We felt intensely responsible for Cameron's safety because he was a disabled child. He had always trusted and depended on us to care for and protect him. Our intentions for Cam's health and safety were perfect. Unfortunately, our decision ultimately cost him his life! Guilt weighed heavily on us. We asked ourselves many questions over and over again: Where had we gone wrong? Had God tried to warn us? Why had we encouraged the doctor to do all the procedures at once? Was the surgery more than Cameron could handle? Why hadn't I, the pediatric nurse, stayed the night with him, instead of asking Dennis to stay? Could I have noticed something wrong and somehow prevented his death? It took a long time for both of us to work through these kinds of guilty feelings and questions. With time we resolved most of our guilt.

Dennis's guilt was more intense than mine. He was lying next to Cam when he died. He had kissed him good night shortly before and was relieved he was resting so well with less pain. Had Cameron tried to call out to him? Should he have noticed something was wrong? Had Cameron aspirated or choked—as one nurse and doctor implied, while his father slept next to him? Why didn't he hear something? How could he ever let go of this painful blame and guilt? He sincerely felt he had let his son down by falling asleep. He cried uncontrollably for hours after. Neither I, the children, nor the bishop could comfort him. For the past fourteen years he and Cam had showered, dressed, brushed teeth, and often shared the same fork. The void and guilt he felt were beyond measure. He was a professional counselor and had helped others through their grief, yet initially he felt lost and unable to help himself.

We had both presented grief workshops and experienced loss and guilt before. We now realized, however, that we had only intellectually understood guilt. The intense emotional pain we were now experiencing was more excruciating than all our prior losses combined. We had no idea that loss and guilt combined, could hurt so deeply and endure for so long.

We also learned through this loss experience that there are no clear-cut answers that fit for everyone when it comes to dealing with and eventually relieving guilt.

Cameron's grandmother also felt guilt and expressed it on several occasions. She wrote the following to me almost eight years after Cameron's death:

"I cry when I realize I was not there for you when Cameron died; to help you with the pain and sorrow. (She was in the MTC preparing for a mission. She took one day off to come to his funeral before leaving for Bolivia.) I also regret I did not pay more attention to Cameron when I would babysit him. I was like 'Martha', concerned with tasks, rather than 'Mary' who paid attention to more important things." (Luke 10:38-42).

Unresolved guilt is not healthy. Yet we all are guilty of making mistakes. "To Err is Human." (5 p. 23). Feelings of regret and guilt need to be expressed and, in some cases, confessed. Then we can let go and forgive ourselves. We witnessed firsthand this healing power in the life of a friend of ours who left her older children to watch her two year old while she went inside her house to answer the phone. While on the phone, her child ran into the street and was killed by an oncoming car. This distraught mother couldn't let go of her guilt until someone finally listened and acknowledged her by saying, "Yes, maybe it wouldn't have happened if you hadn't answered your telephone!"

Another way to avoid or confront unnecessary guilt is to confront it openly and rationally. With this approach we attempt to eliminate any "shoulds" from ours or others vocabulary. (If someone tries to shame us, for instance, with too many "shoulds," we could jokingly respond with, "Don't SHOULD on me!")

FALSE GUILT

Dennis and I have found that in many instances individuals are experiencing false guilt, which is blaming ourselves for events and circumstances that we are not actually responsible for. For example, Dennis believed if he hadn't fallen asleep next to Cam, he could have prevented his death; when in reality Cam died quietly in his sleep with the nurse in the room as well as Dennis.

Guilt may require professional therapy to work through in some circumstances. The grieving process will be less complicated when irrational false guilt is eliminated. It often takes someone on the outside to help us see the reality of our situation and help us view it differently. A poignant example of this challenge is often observed with parents struggling and attempting to deal with the suicide of their child. One such parent asked, "Didn't I instill in my child the will to live?" This type of false guilt repeated over time becomes a negative cognitive message that can complicate and delay recovery. False guilt can often be resolved over time by cognitively expressing healthy and accurate thoughts about ourselves and then by integrating and believing these positive thoughts.

The friends and family of suicide victims generally do best when they come to understand and believe they did all they could, at the time, to be loving and supportive. Their loved one, feeling the depths of despair and the absence of hope, ultimately made the choice to end his or her life.

CONTROL ISSUES

Loss is often what causes us to realize that situations and circumstances in our lives are not always controllable. The realization that we have little or no control over parts of our lives can make us feel vulnerable and afraid. To compensate for this fear, we may attempt to over-control others, especially family members and those we feel concern and responsibility for.

"I know I am driving my husband and children crazy. They claim I expect perfection from them. I become so frustrated when they don't do what I think they should. The need to control is an overpowering force since the death of my loved one. Some of it may be the vulnerability I feel like an overprotective instinct that something else bad might happen. I realize I am actually pushing the people away that I love the most. I feel the same frustration when someone tries to control me. I don't like being told what I should do either."

Whenever we experience stressful feelings we should ask ourselves; "Am I trying to control someone or something that is really outside of my control or is someone trying to control me?

Wendy Ulrich Ph.D., lists a paradox called "Power without Control." Some of the ways we give up our power are by waiting for others to take control, not claiming what we want or need, and by using anger, coercion, threats, withdrawal, or blame. (17)

LONGING, YEARNING, PINING, AND SEARCHING

For many of us, this stage of grief lasts the longest. We miss our old life and how things used to be. The rest of our earth life may seem like a long time to wait before things improve or we see our deceased loved one again. Even though we have faith in eternal life, the spirit world seems far away right now. These thoughts and emotions are normal. We may continue to ponder and ask, "Why me?" We may wish to resolve questions that at first seem to have no satisfying answers. These feelings are common responses to what has happened to us. Even though we have great faith and tap into the power of the gospel, we may still experience many of the painful symptoms associated with the grief process. We may yearn for the way we thought things could and should be. We may search for answers, longing for hope and peace to return into our lives again. We may wonder if we will ever feel any better. We might conclude that we must be going "crazy" or doing something wrong to still be in so much emotional pain. These feelings can be very confusing and may last for a long time. The fear of something else "going wrong" can hang over us. Life just doesn't feel right anymore. During this time, anger, anxiety, and depression can become extremely intense. Everyone thinks we are better, and we hate to admit we're not. Dennis and I found it hard to believe that it may take eighteen to twenty-four months to find relief. (6) Functional recovery with severe losses may take additional years to achieve. Remember, we will never be precisely the same again; this loss and experience has become part of who we are now and will influence our future.

HURT AND CONFUSION

Our friends, relatives, ward members and co-workers may feel uncomfortable around us now. Because of their awkwardness, they may appear to ignore us. They may not understand the intensity and duration of our grief or may feel helpless to console and comfort us. Consequently, individuals often offer cliches or platitudes in an attempt to console us while addressing their own ambivalence. These statements can result in hurt and confusion even when offered by individuals who sincerely want to help. Because others have not had our experiences, it is difficult for them to understand the depth and duration of our grief. (See *cliche* on p. 16, 126, 182, 234)

DISORIENTATION AND DISORGANIZATION

Any traumatic event can cause disorientation and disor-ganization in our lives. We may not be able to concentrate as we use to. We may become forgetful and feel like we're in a fog.

I had a difficult time returning to work at the hospital after Cameron died. At that time I was working one day a week in a pediatric unit. I was usually the charge nurse and it seemed more frightening now to care for very ill babies and children. I felt greater responsibility and vulnerability after coming to know personally the trauma of having a child die. I also felt I had lost some of my ability to focus, remember, and perform certain medical procedures.

WITHDRAWAL, ISOLATION, AND LONELINESS

When we feel no one can understand or respond to our pain, it is common to withdraw and isolate ourselves from community, church, friends, and family. However, withdrawal and isolation are unhealthy if they become permanent reactions to our grief.

We might isolate ourselves to the point of no return. We may refuse help and stop reaching out to others. We may not share our concerns and feelings. With time we might find that no one tries to call or come around any more. This self-imposed isolation may feel safer initially. Yet, with time, we may become lonely, bitter, unable to function or find healing. Gradually we lose our ability to feel joy, interact with or accept help from others.

Chronic loneliness occurs when we feel separated and misunderstood not only by others, but by God. (See Ch. 9)

INTERVENTIONS TO HELP US HEAL EMOTIONALLY

For most, grief work is a work of feelings. If we don't

acknowledge and honestly express our painful emotions, we deprive ourselves of the very purging that permits us to eventually abandon them. It is very draining to keep negative feelings hidden. However, many do. We don't want anyone to know if we are angry at God because loss has shaped the way our lives have turned out. We may not want our bishop, home- or visiting teachers to know that we are harboring negative or bitter feelings as a result of our challenges. Over time, if we continue to hide our negative feelings, we will limit our opportunities to work on them. These suppressed emotions can lead to increased stress, depression, anxiety and physical ailments. The least adaptive coping skills become evident when we avoid our grief, either by not thinking about it or escaping through drugs, alcohol or other addictions. For others, obsessively thinking about their tragedy can be damaging. To maximize our healing, we must find a balance between expression and suppression of our deepest feelings and concerns.

Because our emotions affect our physical and mental health, we need to find opportunities to express them openly and honestly. Dennis and I have used some helpful phrases to help the bereaved understand the importance of feeling and expressing emotions: "Feeling is Healing" (7) and "We must Feel it to Heal it." (8)

We must give ourselves permission to acknowledge all our emotions, regardless of what we are experiencing. Acknowledging emotions is the surest way to master them. Acknowledging and accepting emotions occurs most when they are expressed and validated in a safe and supportive environment. This involves facing the pain and taking the time and effort to process our grief.

Women are generally better at emotionally expressing grief issues than men. Men usually do better sorting out the intellectual details of their loss. Both men and women do best when they utilize appropriate cognitive reasoning, while allowing themselves to express feelings. Those who overly intellectualize their loss may need help transmitting the knowledge and cognitive thinking from their head to their heart.

TALKING

Talking with others can heal our emotional and intellectual symptoms. Attending a support group with those in similar circumstances is often healing, because our emotions are often validated through openly sharing with others.

"It was a comfort to know there were people at the support group who could understand, listen and share. I discovered that what I had been feeling and experiencing was normal. I became educated to the grief process. Much of my needed strength came from the support group."

"Before my loss I had never experienced such grief. I was overwhelmed with all my emotions. I received valuable tips and suggestions on how to cope at the support group. Those in the group validated many of my feelings. It was a safe place where I could share and cry with others who understood my pain because they had experienced a similar loss."

An understanding friend or relative can also lend a listening ear and offer support. Confiding in a spouse or someone who is willing to just be there can be therapeutic. A good listener is often all we need. The best gift anyone can give those in pain is to lend an understanding listening ear. There is also the option of seeking professional therapy. A counselor can often help us sort through the cognitive and emotional issues we are struggling with.

Grief work is the hardest work most of us will ever do.

Some of us have never felt this kind of deep grief and pain before. We might be afraid of the intense emotions we feel. Some may fear they are "going crazy" or "losing their mind" or losing control. We need a safe place to express our concerns and intense emotions.

CRYING

Crying is not the only way that we show emotion or grieve; however, it seems to be beneficial both physically and emotionally. It's been reported that "tears shed during grief have more toxins than do regular tears. Tears actually can be healing." (9 p. 8) Nearly three centuries ago, Dr. Samuel Johnson wrote: "Sorrow that hath no vent in tears, maketh the organs of the body weep." (10)

JOURNALS AND WRITING

Keeping a journal is another self-help tool that allows individuals to process their thoughts and feelings. As members of the Church, we are encouraged to keep personal journals. However, in therapeutic writing, we may not want to save all of our negative thoughts on paper for our descendants! In fact, many individuals use therapeutic journals to remove negative thoughts from their minds by writing the painful words down and then symbolically (or actually) destroying the pages. Individuals can get painful, destructive feelings out on paper rather than harboring them inside. Suppression or stuffing our feelings, on the other hand, can be damaging. We may want to keep a loss journal, for our eyes only. This allows us to express inner thoughts and feelings on paper where we can see them, evaluate them and abandon them if necessary. If we keep track of what we have written, it is often helpful to review and evaluate where we were in the beginning of our experience in relation to where we have progressed after weeks or months of writing therapy. We should be able to see some progress in our healing and a gradual reduction of our negative feelings.

Studies have shown that those who write about their traumatic experiences have fewer illnesses, spend less time off work, require fewer doctor visits and develop a more positive outlook. (11 p. 23) We can heal when we are allowed to write our deepest thoughts, fears and angers. It is often easier to be forthright when we know that we don't necessarily have to share our written utterances with anyone.

The "four A's", often used to resolve anger, can also be used with writing therapy to help heal painful emotions.

1. Admit what we are feeling. Don't stuff, repress or bury it deep inside.

2. Analyze the feeling. Try to determine where the emotion is coming from: the event, medical professionals, judicial system, family, church, friends, God, etc.

3. Act on the feeling through talking, crying, writing, or working to resolve the issues. If we are angry toward someone, we could write a letter expressing our concerns and issues. We don't have to mail our letter; we can burn it or save it for later. Later we may look at the letter or writings and gain added insight and perspective. We should try to focus on acting, not reacting. Thinking is too passive.

4. Abandon or accept the emotions we are feeling. This should help us let go of the anger and disappointment, forgiving ourselves and others. (12)

LETTING GO OF CONTROL

When we find ourselves frustrated, fearful or angry with

those around us who won't do what we desire; we can let go of our need to control. Although we may feel hurt, rejected, and unloved, the more we try to control others, especially our children and spouses, the more they pull away from us.

If we will realize we don't need all the control, our anxieties often leave. In addition, many of those around us will quit resisting our influence and direction. The "power struggles" between ourselves and others will soften as we let go. We are actually more likely to get what we want by letting go of our need to control others.

We can grow and heal by following the Savior and our Father in Heaven's example. They never force us. We are free to choose. Agency was given to us as part of Heavenly Father's plan. (Helaman 14:30, Moses 3:17, 2 Nephi 2:27)

We need to remember the principle of agency while dealing with adults and youth. Some church leaders and parents think they: "...understand the principle of free agency, and how to enforce it!"

When I find myself frustrated with others' behaviors that I can not change or control, I remind myself to "accept, don't expect." This can help me to let go of unrealistic expectations for myself and others. I then can reduce my frustration level and avoid some of the side effects that result from attempting to control circumstances and resistant individuals outside my influence.

If we can be patient with ourselves, love unconditionally, and "let go" of our need to control, we will eventually feel additional peace and freedom. I learned this principle as a teenager. Although my application was somewhat immature and naive, it helped me learn to let go of things outside of my control. As young girls, my best friend and I would walk in the hills behind our homes when we were feeling frustrated with life. We would talk and try to figure out life's challenges. When we couldn't find explanations or felt we couldn't do anything about a particular situation, we would start trying to identify something beneficial or put the problem in "God's hands." We echoed a little cliche, "It's probably for the best." We have since learned that not all of life's challenges outside our control turn out good or for the best, yet this positive mental affirmation and "letting go" of the need to control brought us enhanced mental health and increased faith as adults. This concept is expressed well in one of my father's favorite poems, by Reinhold Niebuhr:

"God grant me the grace to accept with serenity the things that cannot be changed, the courage to change the things which should be changed, and the wisdom to distinguish the one from the other." (13)

Accepting and turning those things we cannot change over to God and "letting go" can bring a great sense of relief. Dennis often says: "It's usually not the situation that causes our stress, but how we view it." Viewing challenges as an opportunity for learning helps us avoid becoming a helpless victim of our situation; however, severe challenges may require professional interventions and years of struggling to reframe, understand and accept.

There also may be times in our lives when we need to use control techniques to help us respond more appropriately. To maintain greater control, try to: Think first, act second, and the appropriate feelings should follow. In crises, most of us respond in the opposite order, allowing our feelings to override our better judgment.

CHANGING OUR "WHYS"

Many ask, "Why did this happen?" (logically/medically), and, "why did this happen, God?" (spiritually) For example, when Cameron died, I wanted to know the medical details of why his heart stopped. I also wanted to know why God allows innocent children to suffer and die, and why did Dennis and I have to feel so much grief?We have learned it may be more helpful to change our "Why" to "What", "When" and "Where". We may never fully understand "Why" something has occurred; however, we can identify when and what has happened, what to do now, and where we can go for help. This technique allows us to reduce our feelings of vulnerability as we regain additional control over our world.

Struggling to deal with her mentally delayed child, Pearl Buck asked, "Why?" And then used her positive attitude to find her own answer:

"Why must this happen to me...to this there could be no answer and there was none...my own resolve shaped into the determination to make meaning out of the meaningless and so provide the answer, though it was of my own making...her life must count." (14 p. 26)

Some have changed their paradigm by asking, "Why not me," instead of, "Why me?"

EXERCISE

Exercise can benefit both our emotional and physical health. It reduces irritability and depression caused by loss and stress. It increases the uptake of serotonin and the release of *endorphins*. These are chemicals in the brain that contribute to our sense of "well-being". In addition, walking or jogging outside with a friend or spouse adds the benefits of the sun (light therapy) and social interaction (talk therapy).

TOUCH and MUSIC THERAPY

Many have found and utilized the healing power of touch. Touch can also be utilized as a relaxation technique. Touch seems to help children emotionally as well as adults. It can reduce stressful feelings while increasing security and self-esteem. Touch can also help couples stay connected during difficult times. (See *marriage* Ch.11)

We can use a combination of massage and music to comfort the bereaved or the terminally ill. Research has shown that the power of touch and music can relax us as much as some pain medications or other anti-anxiety drugs. Touch and massage can become healing tools throughout the process as well as amid stress and adversity.

STRESS MANAGEMENT

If someone has a serious car accident and is hospitalized in an intensive care unit (ICU), we don't expect them to return immediately to work, school, church and other obligations. But, when someone experiences a serious loss, we often cannot see their wounds. We expect them to bounce back and function as usual. It might be helpful if we (and they) consider themselves as though they are in an emotional intensive care unit for a time. We would likely be more patient with them and they would likely take better care of themselves if we acknowledged and encouraged a respite time for emotional healing.

Some have busy lives and experience fulfillment by accomplishing many things. Others think that rushing and doing two or more things at once will help them finish their tasks faster, increase self-esteem and reduce their stress.

However, in most instances these strategies don't help. Some research indicates that trying to think of—or do—more than one thing at a time causes our minds to race and often creates more stress. (15)

Stress management may mean learning to say, "No," and conditioning ourselves to stop and think before always saying, "Yes." This can be hard for active members who want to please and serve others. It may be helpful to tell ourselves that it's okay to let others serve us for a while. There must be a receiver for others to give. At different times in our lives, we will experience both roles.

Relaxation and meditation may help us heal emotionally (see more on p. 97, 101). When we are stressed at work or away from home, we can try the following quick stress management techniques: Count to ten, take a deep breath or leave the situation for a time and take a short walk, preferably in the out-of-doors (light therapy).

LITTLE PLEASURES

It is important, while enduring loss, grief and depression, to continue doing the things that formerly brought joy, happiness and pleasure. This may be as simple as ordering a pizza, watching a movie, play or sporting event.

After Cam's death, Dennis and I continued to do the things our family enjoyed doing prior to his death. This was difficult and we felt guilty at first. However, with time, work, and patience, we slowly began to allow ourselves to laugh, experience joy, and celebrate life once again.

FINDING MEANING

Trying to find a reason or meaning behind what has happened to us may be the greatest struggle we will face. It often takes a combination of grief work, prayer and healthy thought processes to discover our own meaning and reconciliation. We are fortunate to have the gospel and our faith to help us. Remember in the beginning, that experiencing spiritual injury is common, especially as we try to understand why God allowed personal tragedy to take place on our lives.

CHAPTER 6

PHYSICAL SYMPTOMS AND
PHYSICAL INTERVENTIONS

The list of acute physical symptoms caused by loss is extensive (see Figure 3). We may feel physical pain or aching as the shock and numbness wears off. We might experience a tightness or hollowness in our stomach or chest. Breathing difficulties, or a dry mouth, is also common. The heart may pound so fast and hard that we feel we could surely die, or wish we would! We may be restless, unable to sit still, or so weak and exhausted we cannot possibly move. Many experience changes in bowel, appetite, and sleep patterns. Some experience headaches, blurred vision, and nervous twitches.

The immune system is often suppressed when the body is exposed to grief and stress. Individuals experiencing a traumatic situation have a higher incidence of physical illness and death for up to two years after the death of a loved one (1 p. 5). I had a serious eye twitch and abnormal lab tests for two years following Cameron's death. Physicians searched but never found a cause for these conditions. After my own research I felt my physical symptoms may have resulted from the tremendous grief I was experiencing. Physical symptoms may be intensified by any emotional reaction such as guilt, depression, anger, anxiety, resentment, bitterness etc. The majority of individuals seeking medical help and those currently hospitalized present with a history of multiple losses. Thoughts, feelings and attitudes affect our physical health.

HELPING AND HEALING THE PHYSICAL BODY

Physically fit individuals are better able to endure emotional and mental stress. It becomes difficult for us to function or focus when we are in physical pain or suffering from a physical illness. Grief and stress can actually alter brain chemistry and hormones which regulate metabolism, mood, heart rate, digestion and the immune system. (2 p. 10)

"Clearly, our hormonal balance is crucial to our state of mind and any changes in that balance, whether they are caused by endocrine diseases or self-imposed by conditions like stress, can radically alter our mood, behavior, and personality." (2 p. 92)

It would be helpful to have a physical exam after a traumatic or stressful event. The following are physical interventions and lifestyle tools which can make grief recovery optimal.

EXERCISE

Exercise is known to give us more energy and to help us need less sleep. Exercise can actually decrease depression by positively influencing serotonin and endorphin changes in the brain. Exercise also decreases our vulnerability to physical and emotional illness. Yoga and T'ai Chi work on strength, balance, and flexibility. Cardio workouts like running, aerobics, stair-stepping, cycling, swimming, kickboxing, etc. work our cardiovascular system and can produce endorphin boosts. For safety purposes consult a physician concerning the best kind of exercise for you. Cardiovascular exercise is most effective when we raise our maximum heart rate to a target zone of sixty to eighty percent above our resting heart rate. The target heart rate is reduced with age. The goal is to maintain the target rate for approximately twenty to thirty minutes. Remember to warm up and cool down before and after exercise. For best results strive for three to five workout sessions each week. Many individuals have reported additional mood benefits from exercising and walking outside in the sunlight. Research indicates that sunlight and some artificial lights can increase serotonin levels in the brain. The sunlight does not need to be taken through the skin, but actually enters through the iris of the eye. People who live in the northern areas of the world where the daylight hours are shorter often suffer from Seasonal Affective Disorder (SAD). Patients with SAD often sleep up to two hours more during the wintertime.

FOOD

Research has shown that eating right helps to maintain a proper balance in blood sugar levels. Mood and energy levels also respond positively to a balanced diet. Going several hours without nourishment can leave us irritable and sluggish. New evidence suggests that eating carbohydrates can also enhance the re-uptake of serotonin in our brain, giving us a feeling of well-being. (3 p. 107) These changes in brain chemistry can regulate mood in a way similar to antidepressant drugs.

"It may be more than a coincidence that dietary carbohydrates and both major classes of antidepressant drugs, MOI's, and the tricyclic-uptake blockers, are thought to increase the quantity of serotonin present within brain synapses. Perhaps the subjects on carbohydrates are unknowingly self-medicating." (3 p. 109)

Eating right can give us a sense of emotional, mental and physical well-being. The highest serotonin elevators are carbohydrates; fruits, vegetables, and whole grains. If someone is ill or unable to eat correctly, fruit, vegetable, or protein drinks, vitamins, minerals or herbs may be helpful. Always consult a doctor, be aware of side effects, and follow recommended doses.

The Word of Wisdom (D&C 89) offers significant promises if we eat correctly. We were blessed with this revelation long before science could confirm its dietary value.

SLEEP

The quality and quantity of our sleep also affects brain chemistry. When we are experiencing grief or stress, we may sleep too much or too little; either of which can produce fatigue. It is important for us to get back to a normal sleep cycle. Most of us need seven to nine hours of sleep each night. If the following self-help sleep tools do not work, professionals may offer over-the-counter or prescription aides for short durations.

A few simple adjustments to a bedtime routine may help. It is important to unwind before going to bed. Arrange a quiet time before attempting to fall sleep. Try to go to sleep at the same time each night and arise at the same time each morning. Try a warm bath or milk before going to bed. Milk, meat and other proteins contains tryptophan, a natural hormone in the body which usually causes us to feel relaxed or sleepy. (3 p. 109) Avoid exciting television programs or novels before bedtime. If we are having trouble sleeping at night, we should avoid napping during the day. Often we can walk or exercise instead of napping to get rid of that sluggish feeling. A fatigued body requires rest at bedtime. Avoiding coffee, tea, cola or any food containing caffeine several hours before bedtime.

Some medications have side effects that disrupt our

sleep. Sleeping pills, after prolonged use, can disrupt our deep sleep cycle. Some people have found benefits from taking *melatonin*, a natural sleep hormone, or herbs like *valerian*. Be aware of the side effects and follow recommended doses.

Relaxation and meditation can also be used as sleep-aid tools. Instead of counting sheep, we can use concentrative meditation to focus on a word, object or both. This prevents the mind from ruminating on problems or planning the next day's activities. Some individuals meditate best while focusing on their breathing, a candle, or flowing water, and saying a relaxing word like "peace", "sleep", or "calm". We should concentrate on the word, object or our breathing until we fall asleep. We can also use this technique when we wake up in the middle of the night and have a hard time falling back to sleep.

MUSCLE RELAXATION

The following relaxation technique may ease troublesome symptoms during adversity. The first step in this technique involves lying flat on the back and tightening each muscle group throughout the body. Take several deep slow breaths through the nose, exhaling out the mouth while moving the stomach or diaphragm. Next try to tense, tighten, or contract each muscle group one at a time from head to toe, holding them tight while counting to ten. Now, relax each muscle group in the body completely while exhaling. This technique can be done several times while picturing the body sinking deeper and deeper into the bed, until totally relaxed. Relaxation techniques can be used with meditation (concentrating on a image and word). Some claim that this dimming of the sympathetic nervous system relaxes them better than taking an anti-anxiety drug (4).

If, after trying these self-help tools, one still cannot fall asleep, he may need to get up and get something done and quit worrying about the fact that he is currently not able to fall sleep! Some find relief through music or reading. If sleep problems do continue, consult a physician.

Our emotional grief work is a difficult job. After any major loss: "You can only cope with this new reality in doses. You will first come to understand it with your head, and only over...time...will you come to understand it with your heart." (5)

CHAPTER 7

INTELLECTUAL SYMPTOMS AND HEALING

Intellectual grief includes the mental process that we utilize as we attempt to comprehend and understand what has happened to us. We repeatedly ask the same questions over and over again in our minds, trying to make some sense out of what has occurred. Through this mental rumination, we sift through each bit of information in an attempt to intellectually assimilate, grasp or understand the events. This mental repetition is a desperate attempt to consider other solutions that could have altered the outcomes. We may reason and question, "What if I had done this?" or "What if we had gone there?" We mentally search for a different and better conclusion, diagnosis or prognosis. It can become very frightening as the mind tries to regain some control by recreating or replaying parts of an experience. Many feel confused, disorganized or disoriented. Our intense reactions can cause a lack of concentration. We may experience disbelief and denial. These repeated thought processes may eventually help us accept what has actually happened. We will have to make cognitive adjustments to process this new information. It may take days, weeks, or months for the disbelief, denial and shock to completely wear off. However, with time, most of us will slowly begin to comprehend what has happened.

We may become irritable with noise or stimulation. It may be difficult to concentrate on anything except what has happened to us. This preoccupation can lead to absent-mindedness over an extended period of time.

Some of us may also try to intellectualize the details of our loss without allowing and recognizing our feelings or emotions. When we are finally ready to do our "grief work", we may need help transferring this knowledge from our heads to our hearts so we can experience our emotions. We need to "feel it to heal it."

INCONGRUENT GRIEF/ MEN AND WOMEN

Men and women often grieve in the intellectual and emotional dimensions differently. One theory is that the majority of women (not all) are *right-brain dominant*, meaning they generally function more from the brain's right hemisphere which is associated with feelings and emotions. Most men, on the other hand, are *left-brain dominant* and are more likely to be governed by logic and reasoning. Some professionals define grief as *inside* feelings and mourning as the *outward* manifestation of grief. Most men grieve inwardly. Many don't display the outward signs of mourning as easily as women. Women often express themselves through tears. Men often become quiet and stoic. Some men find relief from their grief by keeping busy at work, planning activities and doing many tasks as they attempt to cope with loss. It is important for couples to be aware of specific gender differences during the grief process. Understanding and accepting our differences will help us keep our marriages intact. (See more in Ch. 11.)

INTELLECTUAL HEALING

Generally, it is helpful for us to intellectually understand grief processes and theories. The knowledge of what we are experiencing can help us understand and accept our intense emotions as normal.

We need to take time to think about and sort through all the information we have received after a major loss. It is okay to repeatedly review and analyze the information. With time, acceptance, and cognitive processing we will eventually be able to let our minds rest and experience a degree of mental closure.

MEDITATION

It is important to do some stress reduction when we have so much mental processing going on. We are not going to be able to handle as much stress as we once did. It is important to reduce stress wherever we can for a while. There are times when we have to let our minds rest and say to our brain, "Stop thinking." We can do this with different kinds of relaxation therapies: imagery/visualization, positive self-talk and meditations. When using visualization we can think about a beautiful place or focus on positive thoughts, allowing our mind to rest. Additional kinds of relaxation therapies include Tai Chi or Yoga, which may help settle our racing minds and slow our intellectual processes for a while.

Meditation is a good way to rest the mind from adversity and stress. It helps us to enjoy the moment we are in (mindfulness) rather than dwelling on a painful past or worrying about a vulnerable future. When we are trying to do concentrative meditation, it is helpful if we don't allow the mind to race and wander. We can observe the mind for clues to repressed feelings, or we can try to control where it takes us through concentration or visualization.

After Cameron died, Dennis and I found we weren't able to concentrate and remember things as well as we used to. I finally realized I had to eliminate several of my outside commitments. I just couldn't function like I had prior to our loss. I required significantly more "downtime." I wasn't able to function at my one-day-per week nursing job as well. This took a long time for me to accept. It was another loss for me, one of the many secondary losses that we often experience following a major loss.

BIBLIOTHERAPY

Another helpful tool for our intellectual grieving is reading. We have been encouraged to read our scriptures and other good books. Initially following a loss we may not feel like reading; we may not even be able to concentrate. However, if we keep trying there is a greater chance that the Lord can comfort and speak to us through the scriptures. When we are going through a traumatic loss, we may want to also read the accounts of others who have had similar afflictions and discover what has helped them. Becoming educated in grief processes and recovery can help us recognize normal responses to loss and helpful tools needed for recovery work.

THOUGHT CONTROL

There are times when we need to "put a limit on our worry." We need a break from our grief. Our minds can rest as we concentrate on other issues. We cannot spend every waking hour thinking about our tragedies without becoming totally exhausted. This is not to suggest that we repress our emotions; however, we cannot allow ourselves to think only of our adversity all day long. As our grief or emotions build we can take time to feel, cry, etc., and then try positive thought control to cope with the rest of the day. If it isn't a good time or place to cry, be sad, or have a negative thought, we can try to think, "stop," and replace the sad emotion with another, more positive, thought or action. Remember the following mental exercise: THINK, then ACT, then FEEL. Most of the time, we make the mistake of feeling first and then reacting without cognitively assessing our situations. This exercise helps to change our focus. First we can place a thought in the mind. This should be a positive thought, or something we desire to accomplish. Then we can act on that thought by doing something positive—thinking alone is too passive. Most likely the feelings that follow that action will be positive and healing.

If we find ourselves in a deep black hole of depression, we should evaluate what we have been thinking about. We should ask ourselves, "What have I been telling myself?" We can often trace our depression back to negative thought processes that we need to reframe. It is hard work to talk positively to ourselves, especially when we have traumatic events going on in our lives. It is not easy to alter negative thinking. A professional psychotherapist may help identify why we choose to think the way we do and help us alter some of the erroneous and unhealthy thinking patterns. Dennis has had to remind me often that I am in charge of my thoughts and feelings as well as my behavior. No one can really make me sad or angry, I actually *choose* to feel that way. We can change our feelings and behaviors by altering our thinking. These techniques are not intended to discourage us from doing our emotional grief work. Grief work involves successful cognitive and emotional processes.

POSITIVE ATTITUDE

Positive thought control has been practiced for many centuries and has proven to be a powerful tool when someone needs to lay his emotional grief work aside and focus on something else. Some call this process *positive mental attitude*, and others refer to it as positive thought reconstruction.

Remember, generally it is not the situation that causes our stresses, but how we view them. We may need to completely reframe how we choose to look at a significant event. This will not be possible in the beginning of the grief processes because we usually don't have control over our initial reactions. Reframing is a process that will likely come later. Gina Morgan, a motivational speaker, gives the following example: Growing up she was told repeatedly, "Life is what you make of it." Following a significant personal loss she realized she had no control over some of life's situations. After many years she discovered she had gained knowledge and gifts from her loss experiences. She re-wrote her life statement: "Life is not always what you make it, sometimes life makes something of you." (1999) F. Scott Fitzgerald discovered a similar principle, he said: "Show me a hero, and I'll write you a tragedy."

Steven Covey refers to significant perceptual changes as paradigm shifts. Instead of asking, "Why me?" We might ask, "Why not me?" Why *should* we be spared painful events in our lives? Why shouldn't we learn how to conquer some of life's greatest challenges? Who said that life would be easy? All of us will have painful experiences at times in our lives. Sometimes we get stuck in a helpless victim-role by asking "Why" over and over. This may cause clinical depression or other serious emotional problems to develop. It can be healing to shift our attitudes by deciding to view our challenges as opportunities for growth. Over time, our serious struggles may actually strengthen us and enhance our future coping abilities. A great philosopher once said, "What doesn't kill me, strengthens me."(1) Another great man who discovered this principle, Victor Frankel, survived the Nazi concentration camps. His father, mother, brother and wife died with millions of other Jews in the gas chamber. He later said:

"...they offer sufficient proof that everything can be taken from a man but one thing: the last of the human freedom—to choose one's attitude in any given set of circumstances." (2 p. 75)

Victor Frankel also discovered that everyone experiences some form of suffering, and to survive we must find meaning, not only in life, but in our suffering. He discovered there are purposes in living, suffering and dying. However, he counsels us to avoid attempting to find meaning for others or give answers to someone's "whys". He suggests we focus on discovering our own personal meanings. Latter-day prophets have counseled each of us to seek and receive our own personal revelation.

GRATITUDE THERAPY

Howard W. Hunter talked often about developing an "attitude of gratitude". He encouraged members not to allow the "four D's" to creep into our lives. Doubt, Despair, Depression, Discouragement. With loss and grief we could add a fifth "D", Denial.

"Anyone who imagines that bliss is normal is going to waste a lot of time running around shouting that he has been robbed. The fact is that most putts don't drop, most beef is tough, most children grow up to be just people, most successful marriages require a high degree of mutual tolerance, most jobs are more often dull than otherwise. Life is like an old time rail journey...delays, sidetracks, smoke, dust, cinders and jolts, interspersed only occasionally by beautiful vistas and thrilling bursts of speed. The trick is to thank the Lord for letting you have the ride." (3 p.60)

Gratitude is an attitude that will add strength, humility

and fortitude to our coping abilities. Gratitude can increase our patience. Usually during adversity our patience with everyone, including ourselves, is limited.

Gratitude can soften our hearts and our thoughts. It can cool the flames of adversity that can consume us. Gratitude can help us bear the bitter and find the sweet.

The Book of Mormon tells us that adversity can soften or harden our hearts. (See Alma 62:41) For example, two people can be confronted with the same experience, like the loss of their home through a natural disaster. One will say how blessed they are to be alive and have the chance to start again. The other may ask, "Why did God allow this to happen? My faith was destroyed along with my home."

We might find peace by asking: "What can we learn or gain from this negative experience?" Kahlil Gibran said it another way, "Pain breaks the shell that encloses our understanding."

CHAPTER 8

SOCIAL SYMPTOMS AND INTERVENTIONS FOR HEALING

During a crisis, we may experience grief symptoms that affect our behavior and social interactions. Adversity can affect how we function at work, home, church, and in other situations. We may become unable to perform sufficiently in our social interactions. This can result in additional losses, including our self-esteem. Because our church membership represents a way of life within our community, the loss of healthy LDS social interactions can complicate our grief recovery and increase the duration and depth of our pain and suffering.

We may isolate ourselves from friends, family and ward members trying to protect ourselves from the constant reminder of what we have lost and what others still have. We may feel shame and embarrassment, especially if we are not living up to our own expectations or the expectations of those around us. We may force ourselves to appear "strong", acting as though we are healing rapidly. We may not feel comfortable sharing the details of our painful emotions and circumstances, or fear that others will not understand our pain, or judge us harshly. We feel vulnerable, fearing that more will go wrong.

LOSS OF IDENTITY / SELF ESTEEM

"After my crisis, I lost some of my identity and self-esteem. I tried to feel I was still useful and valuable. I felt that others at church expected me to move on as if nothing had happened. I tried to do this in a variety of ways. I felt lost for a long time."

"One learns about and creates oneself during each moment of awareness. One is continually amalgamating his new learning with his old knowledge about himself and forever integrating it into an ever-changing concept of self. Once basically formed, this concept of self extends outward from ourselves and becomes mostly responsible for our perceptions or impressions of the world and others." (1 p. 183)

"It's safe to say that the self image is the core personality ingredient which directs every aspect of our being. The way we communicate, the way we handle our emotions, the way we behave publicly as well as privately is all a commentary on our image of ourselves..." (2)

We may feel that we have not only experienced a major loss, but that we have also experienced a loss of self or identity. One individual said: "Part of me has died."

Our identities include personal characteristics, body image, talents, and disabilities. Many of our perceptions are learned as we interact with our environments and others. When there are changes in our physical bodies or environments, we have to make emotional, behavioral and mental adjustments. These adjustments may include viewing our own identities differently. Some call this a *redefining of one's self.*

Serious challenges from our childhood or adulthood traumas may cause a loss of our true selves. Abuse and other destructive experiences may cause us to feel unacceptable. We may then resort to "pleasing behaviors" which we hope will secure the love and attention we need. Many professionals refer to these pleasing behaviors as "masks" because they don't accurately portray the true self. (3 p. 57) These individuals may appear emotionally healthy, yet on the inside they are confused, lonely, anxious, or depressed. An *identity crisis* is another term sometimes used to describe this loss of self.

Some who suppress grief may experience a similar loss of self. We try to hurry and appear to be through with our pain by pretending to carry on as usual. Friends and family often contribute to our denial by complimenting us on how strong we seem, or how much faith we must have to recover so quickly. We may continue to project this false self in an attempt to save face and look as strong and healthy as we perceive others believe and want us to be. Some may have to confront past pains that have been hidden away. During psychotherapy, many are able to relive or claim past behaviors and emotions in a safe environment with a competent professional.

Many who become ill or disabled may have to redefine their identities.

"My illness is very minor compared to so many. I try to keep a positive outlook because I still get around so well. I worry about how I will cope if and when I become more confined. I love to be outdoors. I try to walk, swim or do some form of exercise every day. I also have arthritis and pain in my feet, back, and hands. Some days I am pretty pain-free, but most days I ache in one or all three places. I take pain medications, actually anti-inflammatories. I try to keep busy enough that I don't dwell on my disabilities. I am only in my mid-life and fear the future sometimes. I can't do the things I used to do, like work long hours or get by on less sleep. I can't keep the yard and house up as I used to. I don't feel as useful or valuable as I have in the past. Aging has been difficult, psychologically my body image is not as positive as when I was younger. I see young, healthy individuals and feel sad for my loss of youth and health."

With any traumatic loss, we can experience a loss of personal identity. If we have given and sacrificed for another person or cause over time, and that relationship or cause is lost, part of our own identity or self-image may be lost as well. This secondary loss of self can be as debilitating as the primary loss. When Cameron died, I wondered, "What will I do now? Where do I turn?" As I tried to regain or redefine my identity, it seemed more than I could endure at times.

CO-DEPENDENCE

Our identities are strongly linked to the significant others in our lives. When we see them doing things we don't agree with, it can be hard on our own identities or self-esteem. We may even view ourselves negatively. An example of this would be a parent dealing with an extremely rebellious child or an individual attempting to cope with a dysfunctional spouse. Some feel they have personally failed when they are not able to influence or change children or spouse. We may question our own values or self-worth. We may not be able to separate our own identities and behaviors from the actions, attitudes, and values of other family members. This co-dependent behavior causes us to cover up or control the actions of other family members in an attempt to rescue them. The rescuing, hiding, or controlling of negative behaviors is designed to protect both parties. These dependent personality disorders can cause an identity crisis and loss of self esteem for the "Rescuer". Therapy is often needed to stop the co-dependent cycles. Counseling may establish appropriate identity boundaries and eliminate the unhealthy co-dependent characteristics.

We must realize that it is very difficult to change the personalities of those around us. However, we can influence their positive behaviors and characteristics through our actions. We can offer them unconditional love and acceptance. Similarly, the unconditional and unmerited love we receive from our Heavenly Father builds our self-worth.

HEALING TOOLS FOR OUR IDENTITY AND SELF-ESTEEM/ SELF-WORTH

Helping ourselves in the social dimension can be diffi-cult. It may require getting outside our comfort zones and actually accepting other's help. It may also mean eventually reaching out to help someone else. A helpful intervention for many is to join a support group. (see p. 84) Sharing feelings and experiences with others who are also experiencing similar losses is often therapeutic. The impact of friendship and helping others can be a powerful healing tool. Sometimes we need to remind ourselves: "I am not worthless. I am wounded" (4) and, "In spite of our faults and whatever pain we have brought to ourselves and others, we are worthwhile and able to be loved." (6)

SELF-ESTEEM / SELF-WORTH

What exactly are self-esteem and self-worth? How can we develop, build, or maintain them during and after tragedies? Fred Riley, Commissioner for LDS Family Services, defines self-esteem as: "What you DO."

Self-esteem is often based on society's standards of what our behavior or performance should be. Self-esteem often focuses on doing or having things. It is often controlled by the opinions of others. The goal of self-esteem is to impress others in an endless attempt to feel good about ourselves. Personal accomplishments have their place; however, some ill or disabled individuals are physically or otherwise limited in terms of what they can "do". At times we need to remember: "We are human beings, not human *doings*." Also, "Do we have to *do* more to *be* more?" (4) Why do we tell ourselves we aren't enough? Moroni said, "We are whole". (Moroni 8:8)

Brother Riley defines self-worth as: "Who we *are*."

Self-worth is focused more on "being" rather than "doing". Self-worth is gaining confidence, peace, and happiness based on our attitudes and beliefs. Self-worth does not require the opinion or the evaluation of others. It comes from the inside out rather than the outside in. It is based upon who we are deep inside and how we view ourselves. Self-worth requires understanding that our existence is not by chance.

Self-worth acknowledges that we are created with a purpose, and that our goals and aspirations must be character-based to be fully realized. It requires knowing we are children of God!

Even if we are ill, disabled or cannot perform in any way, we still maintain our character and our self-worth. Stephen Covey said, "Internal security simply does not come externally." (5 p.84)

Research indicates that when we feel self-confident, we function better at work, home, and church. We have more friends, and we view our relationships with others more positively. Self-love precedes our ability to love and accept others. If we are critical of ourselves, we project this critical view to others. We also have a tendency to compare our weaknesses with the qualities we think we see in others. Remember, God's love is unmerited, and is not predicated solely on our performance, or what we do. He loves us unconditionally. If we can feel and accept God's unconditional love, we should in turn feel more self-love and self-worth.

"You can't always try to earn love. In its fullest state, it is given freely to you. It is the love that is there in spite of your faults, that you can trust." (6)

When we feel this kind of love it is easier to reach out and love others.

NEGATIVE LABELS

A positive self-concept is important for all of us; how we feel about ourselves influences how we respond to others as well as how we perceive they respond. A poor self-image may set a negative pattern for a lifetime.

It may be helpful to understand that we are in charge of our thoughts and feelings as well as our actions. In reality, no one can make us feel sad or angry; we *choose* to feel that way.

"Through our lives we tend to maintain many unnecessary and burdensome recurring thought and behavior patterns." (7 p. 1).

Often we learned these self-defeating thoughts and behaviors as children. They helped us cope with particular situations in life at the time. Unfortunately, these thoughts and behaviors continue with us long after the original situations changed. These challenging situations from the past can also result in individuals attaching negative labels to themselves. Our children do this also. If they tell themselves something long enough, it can become a self-fulfilling prophecy that results in enduring self-defeating personality beliefs and characteristics. "For as he thinketh in his heart, so is he." (Proverb 23:7). Many of us say, "I've tried it before." "I can't." "I'm afraid." "Others will laugh at me." With work, we can dispel, or even avoid instilling these labels.

Cameron seemed to have developed a strong inner strength or self-worth. When asked, "What would you never change about yourself?" He said, "My name" "What is the most important thing you own?" "My wheelchair." "What is your most important achievement?" "To learn to read." "What are you like on the inside?" "Happy." "If your life ended today what would you like people to say about you?" "Hey, that was a neat kid! He also had a cool wheelchair." "Whom do you love and admire most?" "God, and my mom and dad."

Many nonmembers asked us about Cameron's ability to maintain a positive attitude in spite of his disabilities. We shared our beliefs that his inner self-worth developed because: 1. He believed in God and that God loved and accepted him. 2. He believed he was a child of God. Christ gave us "power to become the sons of God" (John 1:12). "We are the offspring of God." (Acts 17:28,29) "We are the children of God." (Romans 8) 3. He believed he would live again. 4. He believed he would be healed from his disabilities in the next life, 5. He found purpose, meaning, and happiness in his limited existence here on earth.

When he was just two years old, he wanted to pray. Some of his first words were, "I love God," and he would gaze upward. Somehow he grasped these principles as a source of strength and comfort. Dennis and I discovered there is great joy and peace found in the simplest of existences; in just "being".

Dennis seemed to understand the concept of self-worth and was able to focus primarily on "being" rather than "doing." He would go once a week to the school and work with Cameron and his physical therapist. He wrote:

"I appreciated the beautiful grin that was always present

on Cameron's face when I would walk into his classroom. One week's visit had special significance. For weeks the therapist had prepared me for something very special. Cameron was five years old at the time and could only move himself by rolling on the floor. Today he was sitting on a small tricycle with his feet strapped to the pedals. He was positioned in the middle of the school hallway. Slowly, with great effort, he started to move his tricycle toward me! The pleasure, excitement, and pride I felt are impossible to fully describe. Though he had moved only a few inches in my direction, it was the first time in his short life that he had demonstrated his ability to be independently upright and mobile. I realized at that moment that my pride in my son was no less than that of other fathers who had watched their children overcome great challenges and succeed. I knew he would never be the star quarterback for a high school football team, or even compete with his peers in most areas, yet at this moment, I felt joy and pride for a child who was doing his very best to magnify the abilities and talents he personally possessed.

I had seen the same kind of strength and courage with Brian Alexander, a young teen dying of cystic fibrosis. As Brian's bishop I vividly remember talking with him at his bedside as he prepared me for his ultimate and upcoming death and funeral. I remember his concern for others who had healthy bodies and would live long lives. His empathy and concern for them somehow seemed to be intensified rather than diminished by his struggles with life and his upcoming death. I often found myself contrasting the attitude and peace of mind that Brian and Cameron seemed to possess with other "healthy teenagers" who struggle and have great difficulty finding personal peace and happiness.

I reflected on a young man, badly burned, a suicidal patient on a psychiatric unit. Jeff had a difficult time finding any reason to go on with his life. I found myself contrasting the many limitations and physical challenges that Brian and Cameron faced in comparison to the healthy physical body and numerous abilities and talents possessed by Jeff. I wondered why many who seem to possess a bounteous portion of life's greatest opportunities ultimately find themselves discouraged and distraught, feeling their lives are meaningless. It was then that I began to more fully realize the benefits it can make in our lives when we understand the difference between self-esteem and self-worth. How fleeting self-esteem can be. I reflected on the lives of many who had acquired great financial, political, or career successes, yet in the end chose to abruptly end their lives because they seemed to lack true inner peace and worth. The things we do, our physical attributes, and the way we dress all have an impact on how we see ourselves on a daily basis and affect our fragile self-esteem. In contrast, self-worth, which comes from the inside out, is based on who we are and can be permanent. Self-worth is personally internally controlled by those who possess it. Individuals possessing true self-worth are still affected by the loss of friends, possessions, physical health, appearances, etc. Nonetheless, they seem able to find deep within themselves a worth and a value that carry them through difficult times. Unfortunately, much of today's social values are built upon a self-esteem model that focuses on looks, performance, and obtaining possessions. Our attempts to dress and act in prescribed ways are all designed to increase our esteem and value in society's eyes. Sadly, since the ultimate appraisal of how we are doing comes from others, rather than from within, it can be very fleeting. Ultimately our physical talents and possessions will be left behind, and if we do not have internal insight and love of self and others we too may find ourselves lacking the strength to go on in the face of adversity." (8 p.52-3)

CHAPTER 9

HOW WE GRIEVE SPIRITUALLY AND TOOLS FOR HEALING

As church members our spirituality represents the core of our being. Thus, spiritual pain can be at the very heart of our hurt and may constitute the most painful phrase of our grief work. The spiritual circle is purposely placed in the middle of our diagram so that it overlaps all the other dimensions (figure# 3).

"All things unto me are spiritual" (D&C 29:34, Moses 6:63).

Our spirituality is a unique dimension of our faith and religion. It could be defined as our relationship with God and how we relate and communicate with him. Spirituality is influenced by deep feelings, yearnings, and true knowledge that emanates from our thoughts, heart and soul. Belief in an afterlife or spirit world and interest in unworldly affairs are all part of our spirituality. When we fast, pray, read the scriptures, and interact with ward members at church, we are attempting to nourish our spirituality and feel closer to our Heavenly Father.

Spirituality is an integral part of most member's lives. For believing Saints, the gospel is a way of life. It is belief in and companionship with God and Christ that provide the utmost meaning and purpose in our lives.

Religion may be defined differently than spirituality. Religion is where or how we nourish our spirituality. One's religion includes a system of policies, practices, and beliefs.

Many Americans are no longer "at home" in their religious tradition. Some are experiencing a spiritual homelessness. As members of the church it is comforting to know we have a fullness of the Gospel. People continue to join the Savior's Church, looking for "home," while many other churches are experiencing declining memberships. Newsweek published the following statistics relating to church-membership decline between 1965-1990:

U.S.A. Presbyterian Church—(and its two predecessor denominations) from 4.25 million to 2.85 million.

The American Baptist Church—1.3 million to 1.2 million.

Evangelical Lutheran Church—from 5.7 million to 5.2 million.

The United Methodist Church—from 11 million to 8.7 million.

The United Church of Christ—from 2 million to 1.5 million.

The Episcopal Church—from 3.6 million to 2.4 million.

The Disciples of Christ—from 1.9 million to 1 million. (1)

During the same time period, The Church of Jesus Christ of Latter-day Saints grew significantly. In 1960 there were 321 stakes (each stake has approximately three thousand members). By 1991 the number had grown almost six times to eighteen hundred stakes. In 1998 alone, 299,000 converts joined the church while the number of stakes increased to 2,505. The total church membership exceeded 10 million members that same year. (2 4/99, p.78)

The LDS religion, with its emphasis on obedience to God's commandments, requires a lifetime of work and service. As Latter-day Saints we are blessed with revealed spiritual direction that brings meaning and purpose into our lives. Spiritual direction from inspired leaders can also can bring healing and comfort for those experiencing adversity.

SPIRITUAL INJURY

For many bereaved, "God may become the answer and the question." (3) Some may feel as David:

"My God, my God why hast thou forsaken me? Why are thou so far from helping me...? I cry in the daytime, but thou hearest not...' (Psalm 22:1,2) "How long, O Lord? Will you forget me forever?" (Psalm 13: 1)

Moses cried:
"Lord, wherefore hast thou so evil entreated this people? Why is it that thou hast sent me? For since I came to Pharoah to speak in thy name, he hath done evil to this people; neither hast thou delivered thy people at all." (Exodus 5:22-23)

In the beginning of Job's adversity he suffered spiritual injury:
"...Today is my complaint bitter: my stroke is heavier than my groaning...Oh that I knew where I might find him...I would fill my mouth with arguments. I go forward, but he is not there; and backward, but I cannot perceive him." (Job 23:2,3,8)

The Lord didn't immediately answer all of these prophet's questions and concerns, and he may not answer all of ours.

Sometimes adversity influences individuals to turn more completely toward God and their faith, finding comfort and strength. Others confronted with adversity become hurt, confused or angry with God and/or church leaders and members. At times faithful and religious members become hurt spiritually, especially when they thought God would protect or shield them from their adversity. Over time, hurt, confusion and anger can develop into spiritual injury, even among faithful and active church members. Spiritual injury can be defined as feeling alienated from one's previous personal spirituality. It may include a feeling of being separated from God, Christ, or our ward families.

"Why am I hurting, and in so much pain when I have the truth of the Gospel?" "Why did God allow this to happen to me?" "Why was I born this way?" "Haven't I been a good person?" Others may wonder, why God would allow an innocent child to suffer, why he doesn't protect them.

A spiritually injured woman said:

"After my daughter died, my existence shattered. I felt like I had been run through a meat grinder. It has obscured everything in my life, and distorted my view of God and humanity."

It is common for people of all religions to become "Spiritually Injured" during or after tragedies and adversity. It crosses all races, cultures and creeds. Spiritual injury usually results when life's realities contradict and/or conflict with our previously-held spiritual assumptions.

I wrote the following after Cameron's death:

"All my planning, hope and prayers for my son's successful surgery seemed in vain. The neatly-woven incisions on his hips as he lay lifeless, seemed a mockery to all my plans and organization. His new electric wheelchair sat motionless. I knew I had faith, believed in God and in life after death, yet in the beginning, I found my grief so intense that my faith alone was not enough to comfort me."

During adversity some are unable to experience spiritual feelings and question their faith and worthiness. This type of spiritual injury is a common grief response. With time and grief work, most of the spiritually injured will return to their previous faith and beliefs, finding the comfort they seek. It may be necessary to redefine or reframe some of our harmful erroneous beliefs. This healing requires time, prayer and proper grief work.

Some will feel judged at church, fearing that others think they caused or deserved their adversity.

"I thought this kind of thing happened to those who weren't righteous enough. So when it happened to me, I felt ward members were judging me as less worthy."

Others, especially children, promise or bargain with God trying to change their situation:

"I will be good. I'll never do anything wrong. I will pray every day, go to church, if I can just be cured."

One child asked his mother after the death of his sister and in the midst of his own mental illness: "Mom, why do really bad things keep happening to us?" (I worried about this child when, five years later, I got a call reporting that his other sister had been hit by a car and was in a coma.)

Some children and adults plead and pray for a miracle or other types of divine intervention. Others fast, pray and receive priesthood blessings.

"I prayed as a young child that God would not let my parents get a temple divorce. After their divorce, it took me a long time to understand why he did not answer my prayer the way I wanted."

Some feel shame and discouragement when they hear others bear testimony of how their prayers were answered, or express how they were protected, warned or healed because of their faith and or obedience. We may question within ourselves, "Why wasn't I warned, protected, or healed, or why didn't I receive a miracle? "We may wonder what is wrong in our lives, blaming ourselves as we question our faith or worthiness.

"I knew if I just prayed hard and believed, God would make me well again. It's been so hard to understand why he hasn't. Doesn't he love me? Aren't I righteous enough? Am I being punished? Is my faith weak?"

After a loss or tragedy some return to the church looking for and finding comfort in the hymns and lessons. The same hymns and lessons cause others to remember and long for what they have lost. This in turn may cause them to suffer deeper feelings of loss and spiritual injury. Many are:

"Astonished to note their own feelings of anger at a scripture reading regarding the resurrection and healing, sadness at stories—scriptural or otherwise—of tenderness or loss, depression regarding a flashing of memory..., hurt and envy at the announcement of others going on with their lives with baptisms, confirmations, and marriages, and indignation when a reference is made to the justice and mercy of God. These feelings are often exacerbated by familiar, meaningful songs and music that cause the spill-over of tears again and again." (4 p.127)

A friend and bereaved woman at a regional conference heard an area authority comment on the many miracles he had observed among the stakes. He concluded that the members were very faithful and strong.

She wrote:

"I thought, 'Why couldn't my family have been one of those miracles?' I had to leave the meeting early because I couldn't stop crying. I realize that everything can't be a miracle, but it is hard not to look at other's miracles around you and not wish for one, too. My mind knows better, but my heart still hurts."

Other faithful members are ashamed to express their doubts and questions:

"Often people are embarrassed by their questions, as though they should have the answers themselves already, or should have learned them in church or in the common culture, and are ashamed that they obviously weren't listening the day these issues were discussed. Sometimes they feel intimidated, fearful that if they ask the questions on their minds, God would punish them for their unbelief or their theological stupidity. So they wander in agonizing silence, ashamed and afraid, yet forever unsettled by the nagging, nonsequiturs called forth by trying to align their experience of loss with the scriptures they read and the sermons they hear." (4 p.143)

A former bishop, stake president, and mission president revealed the depth of his anguish twenty years after the death of his daughter:

"Did this happen because I didn't have enough faith? Was it something I did? Wasn't I worthy enough to have prevented it?"

He, like many, still asks himself these same painful questions over and over. His anguish validates the lifelong grieving most parents experience after losing a child. He also shared somewhat reluctantly, "I send her love daily."

Others question whether they are stuck in their grief work or lack sufficient faith to move forward.

"I asked the same questions over and over. Then I think I've resolved them in my mind, only to find myself asking them again."

This constant questioning of one's faith and worthiness can result in spiritual injury.

A sexually abused child wondered and questioned:

"I prayed that God would stop him from coming into my room at night. When he continued to come and sexually abuse me I wondered, ' Is it because I am bad?'"

Others experience confusion, disappointment and guilt that can contribute to their spiritual injury:

"I still can't believe my temple marriage is over. Why didn't God intervene? I knew God could and I believed that he would."

Occasionally members feel that their personal world has crumbled, and they fear that God is no longer with them or has failed to care about and protect them. These fears and disappointments can complicate the grief process and cause spiritual injury.

Often church leaders and well-meaning members are at a loss and find it difficult to accept and support those experiencing chronic suffering. They do much to comfort and provide support to families during the initial crises or illness, at the funeral, and for several weeks thereafter. The outpouring of meals, service, personal attention, and love are appropriate and usually greatly appreciated. Unfortunately, most ward members are not as aware or comfortable with the realization that the mourning and recovery from a significant loss may last months and often years. They don't realize or want to believe that some will never fully get over their loss and, in fact, may desperately need continued support to endure and get through their personal Gethsemanes.

Those of us in mourning often feel unaccepted, confused, or judged. We fear that if we don't heal quickly, we may be considered weak, unworthy, or unfaithful. As we pull away from significant others we add guilt to our list of negative emotions. We may fear that we are not only turning from ward members and our faith but also from God. Because having faith is a sense of belonging to God and is often felt through God's leaders and servants, we may feel painful spiritual rejection during our grief. Our self-imposed isolation, compounded by our negative emotions, is usually of no benefit to ourselves or anyone else. There are, fortunately, countless examples of church leaders that have responded with charity, empathy and understanding:

"Why, when I hurt the most, did God seem silent?" Her spiritual leader replied, "It is hard to hear the still, small voice when your soul is screaming in pain." (5)

The Book of Mormon describes two different kinds of reactions we may have following affliction:

"But behold,...many had become hardened,...and many were softened because of their afflictions, insomuch that they did humble themselves before God, even in the depth of humility." (Alma 62:41)

Despite good intentions, our reactions and feelings in the face of tragedy may be difficult to control. Most of us would choose the latter response—to be softened. However, when tragedy hits, our good intentions may leave. We may feel

shame and wonder what is wrong for having such negative feelings. This is how spiritual injury can begin.

We can contribute to another's spiritual injury through
the comments we make. We sometimes innocently share opinions or cliches without thinking ahead about how our
platitudes may affect those who are mourning.

"I finally went through my angry stage of grief. I have a
close friend at church who said, At least your new trial has
probably taken the focus off of your grief for your daughter's
death. She will never know just how wrong she was! I think of
you constantly, of your normal birth, of how healthy you were.
How you offset the pain we sometimes feel with your brother's
disability. I am so angry you had to die. I wouldn't be going
through any of this if you were alive. My faith has wavered!" (6
p.132)

RELIGIOUS CLICHES

Religious cliches, like secular cliches, can cause additional hurt, anger, sadness and guilt. Often we use them
because we don't know what else to say. These statements seem
to readily come to our memory. We need to be careful when
using doctrinal cliches or phrases that may cause or increase
spiritual injury.

Possible examples include:

1. It's God's will.
2. If you have enough faith you will be healed.
3. God will heal him.
4. There is a reason for everything.
5. You don't die until your time is up.
6. Count your blessings.
7. God took him or her.

8. Only the good die young.

9. Your loved one is freed of this terrible world.

10. You have an angel in Heaven.

11. God doesn't give us more than we can bear.

12. Keep the faith.

13. God needed or wanted her.

Even if we believe some of these cliches, individuals often feel as if we are trying to diminish or negate their pain and grief when we share them. We can't take their grief away. Most individuals need to search out their own revelations and answers, rather than hear our thoughts or sermons, especially in the early stages of loss and crisis. Remember that possessing strong faith doesn't necessarily mean there is less of a need to grieve, and weak faith doesn't always correlate with intense grief. (For supportive comments refer to Ch. 13.)

We can also help those grieving by educating others who have made such remarks. With understanding and love we will be better prepared to reach out to those in grief without causing the bereaved to question their own spirituality or experience negative feelings. Spiritual growth will be enhanced as individuals come to understand and accept the grief process, its duration, and, most importantly, its compatibility with faith and spirituality.

TOOLS FOR SPIRITUAL HEALING

Christ is a "man of sorrows, and acquainted with grief." (Isaiah 53:3)

Adversity visits all who walk this earth including faithful, worthy Latter-day Saints. How can we prevent the negative things that happen to us from doing negative things *to* us? We are less likely to become negative and overwhelmed if we can focus on God, the source and author of spiritual tools. He gave us the Atonement through his son and the gift of the Holy Ghost as His voice. He is a comforter and the revealer of truth. Those things that bring spiritual healing come through Godly sources. Revealed truth and faith in the atonement will not cause spiritual injury or "enlarge the wounds of those already wounded." (Jacob 2:9) The painful trials and tribulations of earth life are, of course, part of the experience God provided for each of us. We agreed to all the conditions of our mortal existence.

"...the sufferings of this present time are not worthy to be compared with the glory which shall be revealed in us." (Romans 8:18)

Many bereaved members have found that healing from spiritual injury occurs when they feel safe to express their fear, anger, and doubt. A mother whose daughter died of cancer said, "I may not know what I believe about God any longer." The following insight, love and acceptance expressed by her church leader helped her through the healing process: "God can handle your anger, fear and doubt. You are not the only person to ever question your beliefs during tragedy." What a relief for this woman and those experiencing spiritual injury to find someone willing to listen and accept their confusion and pain without condemning judgment. She was then better able to start the process of spiritual healing and forgiveness. With unconditional love and support, many will start to nourish their faith again by returning to prayer, scripture reading, and church attendance. Most will heal and return to their faith with time, patience and grief work.

"After my tragedy, I had to start all over again with my testimony and beliefs. At first I wouldn't allow myself to read LDS doctrine or from the Book of Mormon. I wanted to learn what others believed. I read and studied from many books, including the Bible. Slowly my spiritual pain improved and I returned to my own faith, doctrine, and the Book of Mormon."

A woman who was angry at God said:
"If I didn't believe in God, I wouldn't be angry at him now for not protecting me from this tragedy."

Belief in God allows us to access His power and comfort. Those who ask, "Where is God?" in such a crisis may need to open their hearts to find him. After expressing confusion and anger, many will be able to let go of their fears and look again to Him.

"The spirituality of grief requires us to turn inward, to go deep into the wilderness of our soul. We may have to feel depression and anxiety. There is usually no quick way out. We may feel like we are drowning and have to tread water. We must realize disorder and confusion are part of the journey. *Healing the soul* becomes *managing the soul*. Let sadness show you what happiness is, let happiness show you where sadness was. Growth may mean change. Sometimes you can only handle pain in doses. You may find a new inner balance with no end point. Growth means exploring our own assumptions about life. You can't control the wind on a boat, but you can adjust the sails. Tragedies challenge us to look at our assumptions about life. We must pay attention to the spirit. You can reframe your beliefs within your own religion. You can be death-accepting versus death-denying. Learn where you go when you hurt and what brings you comfort." (7)

RECONCILING FAITH, PAIN AND GRIEF

After Cameron's death, I was confused because I thought

that if I had enough faith it wouldn't hurt so badly. I believed I would be shielded from most of the painful feelings of grief. I came to realize there is a difference between grieving and having faith.

Dennis and I found many other deeply faithful church members who wondered why they were feeling such profound pain when they had been obedient and faithful. Some have been referred to 1 Cor 10:13 which says, "God will not suffer you to be tempted above that ye are able to...escape or bear it." Also, in Alma 13:28-29 it cautions us to watch and pray "that ye may not be tempted above that which ye can bear." Some have interpreted this to mean that they would not be given more challenges than they could handle. The scriptures use the word temptation, which may have a different connotation, "tempted more than we have strength to resist." It may have more to do with sin rather than adversity, pain and grief. We have met many who feel they are barely hanging on; some become suicidal. Other individuals give into temptation and sin; however, it is generally not our place to judge whether or not they had the emotional or mental strength to resist their personal temptations. During adversity, individuals may feel like giving up and, unfortunately, some do have mental or emotional breakdowns and ultimately do give up. Only God knows what their mental, physical and spiritual states are. For most of us it is simply helpful to understand that exercising faith and experiencing grief represent two important yet uniquely diverse issues. Mourning for our loss does not necessarily mean we are weak or that we have lost our faith. Grieving, crying and feeling pain for our situation is not conclusive evidence that we don't have sufficient faith or are weak. We can believe in God, life after death, and all the truths of the gospel and still experience profound pain, grief and sadness in our mortal lives.

It is also common to question God and some of our previous beliefs during the grief process. Some have embraced false interpretations of doctrine that should be altered and reframed. This is especially difficult if these false beliefs or traditions were ingrained through reinforcement by our parents or other significant individuals. The following scriptures discuss how the traditions of our fathers influence us: Mosiah 1:5, Matt. 7:8, Alma 3:8, Alma 9:16.

"My mother taught me I would be protected and blessed if I lived the Gospel. I interpreted this to mean that because I was a member of the LDS church living all the commandments, this tragedy would never happen to me."

It is helpful to understand that being protected and blessed doesn't mean being exempt from trials. It does mean we can receive direction and be strengthened to endure our trials in ways similar to Christ, Joseph Smith and other prophets. It might be well to remind ourselves that we will "...receive no witness until after the trial of your faith." (Ether 12:6)

It is important for those experiencing trials to understand that there is a difference between faith and our need to grieve or feel sad. Understanding this truth can relieve our guilt and allow us to feel God's love.

Attempting to console those who have lost loved ones or endured serious trials by saying it will be better in the next life tends to minimize their immediate pain: "It's like you're on a desert and you are dying of thirst, and someone says, 'Yes, you can have a drink, but not for thirty years!'" (8 p.151)

Yes, we will see our loved ones again and we will be relieved from our adversities in the next life. However, that ultimate destination for many of us follows a long, painful, earthly journey! We can develop "patience in tribulation,"

(Romans 5:3-4, D&C 54:10) and maintain faith even as we experience intense grief. God comforts us by reminding us that in his time, "afflictions are but a moment." (2 Cor 4:17-18)

MIRACLES AND AGENCY

It is healing for us to believe that God can and does intervene in our lives, and that miracles do happen. "God has not ceased to be a God of miracles." (Mormon 9:15), and "Miracles have not ceased." (Moroni 7:27-29, Mormon 9:19) It can be equally healing to understand that in most instances, God allows natural laws to run their course. Many will have to endure earth life with significant illness, disabilities, loss and emotional pain. Our miracle or healing may not occur in this life and "Our faith will be tried." (3 Nephi 26:11)

Often we refer to miracles as a guaranteed predictable event when they are, in reality, a hoped-for occasional example of how God can work in our lives. Sometimes we forget that major miracles in the face of life's tragedies are the exception rather than the rule on our earthly journey. In the shooting tragedy of Columbine High School and bombing of the Oklahoma Federal Building, many asked why some victims survived and others did not. Some of those interviewed said, "We are grateful that God protected and spared our lives." Consider the unsaid message to those who had lost loved ones. This may sound harsh; however, what many of them heard was, "God did not protect our loved ones, or we were not blessed". The same illustration could apply to other kinds of loss and adversity. A bereavement counselor interviewed many people after the bombing. He concluded that those who were coping well believed that God did not cause or intend this horrible event and that God was in fact grieving with them. Those who were not coping as well believed that God controls and plans everything, and thus was responsible for the bombing and the deaths of their loved ones.

Many have asked, "Why does God allow good, innocent men, women, and children to suffer?" If their suffering is caused by someone else, it is helpful to explain that God generally does not take away another individual's agency. God allows choice. (Alma 60:13) Evil individuals can and do hurt and murder other innocent victims who are living gospel centered lives.

Moral agency is an important doctrine and principle of the Gospel. It was Satan's plan to destroy our agency. With their agency, some choose to make poor choices, to sin, and even slay innocent victims. In the Book of Mormon, Alma and Amulek watched as faithful believers were burned. Amulek wanted to use God's power to save them. Alma said:

"The spirit constraineth me...the Lord receiveth them unto himself, in glory; and he doth suffer that the people may do this thing...that the judgements which he shall exercise upon them in his wrath would be just; and the blood of the innocent shall stand as a witness against them." (Alma 14:11)

Moroni's teaching illustrates that to ensure God's justice and judgment the Lord at times permits righteous individuals to suffer or die as a result of another's sinful use of agency, "His justice and judgment may come upon the wicked." (Alma 60:13)

Although we are free to choose our actions, responses, attitudes, etc., we are not free to choose the consequences and, "Man is not free to determine truth...." (9 p.160)

GOD COMFORTS

God is there to comfort and support us through our trials: "I will come to you." "I will not leave you comfortless."

(John 14:18) "The word of God heals the wounded soul." (Jacob 2: 8-9)

"But behold, I, Jacob, would speak unto you that are pure in heart. Look unto God with firmness of mind, and pray unto him with exceeding faith, and he will console you in your afflictions, and he will plead your cause, and send down justice upon those who seek your destruction." (Jacob 3:1)

"...He hath sent me to bind up the broken hearted,...to comfort all that mourn; to appoint unto them that mourn in Zion, to give unto them beauty for ashes, the oil of joy for mourning, the garment of praise for the spirit of heaviness; that they might be called trees of righteousness, the planting of the Lord, that He might be glorified." (Isaiah 61:1-3)

It is comforting to know that God "hears us in our affliction" (Alma 33:11), and that He "will wipe away our tears" (Rev. 7:13-17). Although we may not understand why some of us are healed and others not, it is comforting to know He does have the power to heal us physically, mentally and spiritually. He will "take upon him...the sicknesses of his people" (Alma 7: 11) and He will "...succor us in our weaknesses." (Alma 7:12)

JUSTICE and MERCY

John Taylor wrote:
"There may be circumstances arise in this world to pervert for a season the order of God, to change the designs of the Most High, apparently, for the time being. Yet they will ultimately roll back into their proper place—justice will have its place, and so will Mercy, and every man and woman will yet stand in their true position before God." (10 p.346)

Mortal life can seem endless for those facing long-term adversity. Earth life is not fair. Elder Maxwell reminds us: "If it's fair, it is not a true trial." (11 p. 31.) Our hope in the gospel is that the accountability and judgment of God will make things equitable in the eternities.

It can be helpful for innocent victims to know that God is just and merciful and that there will be a punishment for those who use their agency inappropriately. The principle of God punishing the wicked is taught throughout the scriptures: "The wages of sin are death." (Romans 6:23) Spiritual death is separation from God. Also, the Lord will judge and punish the unjust. (Deut. 24:16, 2 Peter 2:4) Additional examples of punishment for sin are found in the Book of Mormon: 2 Nephi 2:5, Mosiah 2:33, Mormon 4:5, and Alma 42:22.

WHY ME? WHY NOW? WHY THIS WAY?

The following was written by a mother who lost her teenager to a bike/truck accident. This is a letter to her deceased son. It displays the common confusion and questions:

"...I love you so. I'm so sorry that I wasn't there that morning, to not let you ride, for not making you go with me that terrible day. I love you so much. All I want for you is to be happy. Please, please be happy. Please be with us in Eternal Life. Was this the way it was supposed to be?"

The "whys" are a common and painful part of adversity. We ask them over and over again. We think we have finally resolved them, and then we ask again. There seems to be two kinds of "whys": Why did this happen, God? And "Why" did this happen logically, psychologically or medically? Many have found, "He who has a *Why* to live for can endure almost any *How.*" (28) The irony of our *Whys* are: "How often in happy times did you ask, "Why?" (12)

There are some theological answers to the "why me?" questions in the scriptures. We must, however, be careful not to overuse these interpretations. Scripture reading and gospel study shared at the appropriate moment can be therapeutic and comforting. At the same time, we need to be cautious and throw out false doctrine which may be culturally-based on traditions rather than the Gospel.

Elder Neal Maxwell explains that trials come to us from three general categories (11 p.29-31): Type l: Trials we bring on ourselves by the sinful choices and mistakes we make. (Often we blame God for our trials and overly identify with Job, when in actuality our trial is self-imposed.) Type ll: Trials that are part of earth life. For example, people get sick, have accidents, endure old age and die. We could also add to this category those who suffer innocently from the sinful choices of others. Those abused, murdered, betrayed, etc. Type lll: Trials God uses to refine us: "But he knoweth the way that I take: when He hath tried me, I shall come forth as gold." (Job 23: 10) When Christ was asked if a man's blindness was the result of sin, he answered: "Neither hath this man sinned, nor his parents but that the works of God should be made manifest in him." (John 9:1)

It is not our place to decide which of the three types of adversity our neighbors are experiencing. Our tendency to judge others is humorously illustrated in the following definitions: Punishing: What the Lord is doing to your Gentile neighbor when misfortunes come. Chastening: What the Lord is doing to your LDS neighbor when adversity hits. Testing: What the Lord is doing when a bad thing happens to you. The will of the Lord: The reason I am rich and you are poor. Bad luck: The reason why you are rich and I am poor. (Saintspeak)

"Judge not that ye be not judged." (Matt. 7:1)

It is helpful to remember that at times in their adversity, Job, Moses, David, Joseph in Egypt, Joseph Smith, Jesus and many other righteous servants have felt forsaken by God during their suffering. At times it may be difficult for us to understand why God doesn't intervene the way we think is best. When Shadrach, Meshach, and Abednego were to be thrown into a "burning fiery furnace", they displayed their commitment and faith by replying: "Our God whom we serve is able to deliver us....BUT IF NOT, be it known...that we will not serve thy gods, nor worship the golden image..." (Daniel 3:7-8)

President Kimball, while a member of the Council of the Twelve, authored a pamphlet called, "*Tragedy or Destiny*". He humbly cautions that the pamphlet contains many of his own thoughts and personal beliefs; nevertheless, Elder Kimball's personal revelation is insightful and poses some challenging questions for each of us to ponder. He asks, "Does the Lord cause tragedies in people's lives?" He questions, "Why does the Lord let these terrible things happen?" A child was drowned, several people were killed in a plane crash, a young elder was killed in the mission field. Elder Kimball asks, "Was it the Lord who directed the plane to crash or the drowning to occur?" He raises the question, "Could the Lord have prevented these tragedies?" He confirms that the answer is definitely, yes, the Lord is omnipotent with all power. However, he poses additional questions, "What if the Lord always punished the wicked and blessed the righteous?" How would the gospel law of moral agency work? Wouldn't we always choose righteousness if we were immediately blessed? Wouldn't the wicked choose righteousness if they were immediately punished? Would they continue to choose to be wicked? Should the righteous be protected from hardship, pain, suffering, sacrifice or tragedy? Pres. Kimball shares:

> "But if all the sick were healed, if all the righteous were protected and the wicked destroyed, the whole program of the Father would be annulled and the basic principal of the gospel, free agency, would be ended. If pain, sorrow and total punishment immediately followed the doing of evil, no soul would repeat a misdeed. If joy, peace and rewards were instantaneously given to the doer of good, there would be no evil—all would do good and not because of the rightness of doing good, there would be no test of strength, no development of character, no growth of powers, no free agency, only satanic controls. Should all prayers be immediately answered according to our selfish desires and our limited understanding, then there would be little or no suffering, sorrow, disappointment or even death, and if these were not there would also be an absence of joy, success, resurrection, eternal life and Godhood." (13 and 27 p.97)

Would we have protected Paul from his "thorn in the flesh"? The Lord said unto him, "My grace is sufficient for thee: for my strength is made perfect in weakness. Most gladly therefore will I rather glory in my infirmities that the power of Christ may rest upon me." (2 Cor. 12: 7, 9-10)

Would we have allowed Jesus to stay on the cross? Would we have allowed the Prophet Joseph Smith to suffer in Liberty Jail, and later die in the Carthage Jail if we had all power?

At times when we ask "Why," what are we really saying?

"Lord, let me be in control, give me the reins, everything will work out better if I'm in control. I doubt God's goodness because He does not use His power exactly as I wish." (14 p.3)

> My life is but a weaving between my God and me
> I let him choose the colors, He worketh steadily.
> Oft times he worketh sorrow and I within my heart forget
> He sees the pattern while I see only part.
> The dark threads were as needful in the weavers skillful hand
> As the threads of gold and silver in the pattern He had planned.
> Not till the loom is silent and the shuttle ceases to fly
> Shall God unroll the canvas and explain the reason why.

(15)

GOD'S WILL

One mother asked, "Was it 'God's will' that my daughter was raped and murdered?" Many hurting members have struggled when they were told their adversity is "God's will". It seems helpful when Dennis and I say to them, "It is certainly God's will that we experience earth life and return to him. God created this world where we experience pain, sickness, accidents and death." However, to say to the suffering individual that God's finger was on the trigger or that he caused someone to be murdered, raped, abused or betrayed "...is a cruel and unreasonable false doctrine." (4)

"I have seen people in the hospital with injuries or illnesses who accept this is God's will. Sometimes we can say, 'I wonder what kind of God would specifically cause a person to injure their knee or get cancer?' That helps the person realize 'Oh, I don't think God CAUSED this' thus opening a discussion of how God may have allowed us to come to earth and allowed these things to happen to us but did not directly cause this." (16 p.20)

WORTHINESS / PUNISHMENT AND GRIEF

It is helpful to understand the interrelatedness between worthiness, pain and grief. Many people believe their tragedy is a punishment for past sins. Belated confessions to extramarital affairs, church inactivity, breaking commandments, and dishonesty, are common when personal tragedy occurs. These shortcomings often come quickly to mind when life's circumstances seem out of our control. It may come from being taught that if we play with fire we will get burned. If we fail to look both ways when crossing the street, we could be hit by cars. If we cheat, lie or steal, we will someday have to pay for those choices. When we receive blessings from God, it is through obedience to eternal laws. (D&C 130:20-21) Conversely, some of us may inevitably reason that when we don't receive blessings or protection from God, it is always a result of our personal weakness and sin. After a crisis, these and other perceived truisms quickly flood our minds, complicating our grieving. We may search for some wrong we did in the past to explain our present loss. The association of loss and shortcomings may actually increase the complexity of our grief process. However, if our adversity is indeed a result of sin then it is important that we use the repentance process as a healing tool. As we confront adversity, we must evaluate each situation and, when appropriate, eliminate incorrect and erroneous thinking. When we come to understand that "God maketh his sun rise on the evil and on the good" (3 Nephi 12:45) and that in reality it "rains on the just and the unjust" (Matt. 5:45); We are then more likely to acknowledge and accept that "bad things do happen to good people."(17) With these spiritual insights, we are also more apt to find meaning in our personal suffering.

"Many assume that God personally pulls strings and causes many of these events and it makes more theological sense to say that life is unfair and that God promises to be with us through all of these events. God's power is found in presence, (and in the comfort of the Holy Ghost) not in prevention or punishment." (4 p.144)

As we evaluate ours and others' trials, it might be well to ask:

"... is the reason to teach us a lesson, or provide a situation of suffering, disability, or death, for the specific edification and spiritual growth of another person? To assume this is not only to assume a God of meanness and cruelty, it is also to show incredible narcissism and religious self-righteousness disguised as piety on the part of the person who is not sick or afflicted." (4 p. 145)

"Would God punish or teach me by causing my daughter to experience abuse, my wife to get cancer, or my child to die, or does he allow these events and provide the resources and support necessary for our personalized growth and development toward Godhood?"

Joseph Smith said:

"It is an unhallowed principle to say that such and such have transgressed because they have been preyed upon by disease or death, for all flesh is subject to death and the Savior has said, 'Judge not' lest 'ye be judged.'" (18 p. 15.)

"When one understands that trials are not necessarily the result of one's own doing, the test may be easier to endure." (30 & Mosiah 23:21)

Many righteous individuals, striving to live the commandments, ask, "Did I deserve or need this experience?"

REFINING

We should be hesitant in telling someone God is refining them like Job. Examples in the scriptures of how God uses trails and affliction in specific instances may not represent a sampling of how most of life's trials originate. "...I will refine them as silver is refined, and will try them as gold is tried..." (Zech. 13:11) "For whom the Lord loveth he chasteneth, and scourgeth every son whom he receiveth." (Hebrews 12:6) "Nevertheless the Lord seeth fit to chasten his people; yea, he trieth their patience and their faith." (Mosiah 23:21) He chastens with afflictions (Helaman 12:3) and tries your faith. (Mosiah 23:21)

Elder Neal Maxwell explains that God may not give us the trial; he may just decline to remove it. (11 p.31) If we can be patient and endure, the Lord can "Consecrate our (thine) affliction" (2 Ne 2:2) and support us in our trials. (Alma 36:3)

TESTING/TRYING

Some have also answered their "why me" questions by concluding that God is testing them, trying to see what they are made of. The previous conclusions could apply. Certainly we believe that all life has meaning, purpose and is a test. But should we look to God for inflicting every challenge or thorny problem directly on us as an assignment from him, or are most of our trials a result of living in a world where adversity exists?

Some members are offended when, during a crisis, they are told that God is trying to "tell them or teach them something". God does allow us to learn and grow through adversity, however, making God responsible for causing divorce, accidents, or inflicting illness may result in serious spiritual injury.

"It doesn't seem fair that one would have to guess what God's intended lessons must be. What kind of a God would choose a brain tumor as a learning device? Do you really think God would bestow cancer upon your child in order to teach you something?" (16 p.21)

I had a nonmember client in her late twenties who was sure that the two miscarriages following her marriage were a direct punishment from God. She reasoned that because she had an abortion as a sixteen-year-old youth, she needed chastisement. She also carried a lot of guilt because she had never told her parents about the abortion. The repentance process proved healing for her and she eventually did have a full-term healthy baby. However, the question remained, was her miscarriage inflicted on her because of her sin, or had the abortion she chose caused physical damage to her body that resulted in her compromised ability to maintain a pregnancy?

REPENTANCE / THE ATONEMENT

The previously-mentioned client's crisis encouraged her to go through the repentance process and experience God's forgiveness. "If we confess...God will forgive... ." (1 John 1:9) If we don't repent, God is slow to answer our prayers and deliver us from afflictions. (Mosiah 11:23-25) "We can be turned into another man." (1 Samuel 10:6-9) and receive a new heart." "Faith with repentance bringeth a change of heart." (Hel. 15:7)

Elder Packer shares a beautiful parable of the atonement, repentance, justice and mercy. He tells of a man who wanted more material things than he could afford to buy. He promised his creditor that he would work hard and pay his debt off slowly with time. However, when the deadline came, he was lacking. He could not pay. The creditor put chains on his hands and feet and prepared to send him off to prison. As he was crying and mourning the justice of his fate, a compassionate friend stepped forward, offering the debtor mercy by paying his debt. The chains were removed and he was told he was free to go. With gratitude he agreed to finish paying his debt to this new creditor who had shown him mercy. The allegory is that in spite of all we do we are all lacking and come up short until Christ steps in to pay our debt through the atonement as we repent. (19 p. 54-56)

Christ suffered "the pains of every living creature, both men, women, and children... ." (2 Nephi 9:21). This suffering is not just limited to sin, "but also the cumulative burden of all depression, all loneliness, all sorrow... ." (20 p.104) He has felt the pain and suffering brought about by living single, losing loved ones, facing illness, disabilities, divorce or any of life's losses. He bears all these burdens and is the Savior who understands our every suffering.

"In all their affliction, he was afflicted, and the angel of his presence saved them: in his love and in his pity, he redeemed them, and carried them..." (Isaiah 63:9)

FORGIVENESS

As we hope for God's forgiveness through his atonement, we may need to also offer forgiveness to others or ourselves. Many of our struggles may be related to someone who has hurt us. "Forgiveness can increase emotional and physical healing. Being unwilling to forgive can 'FREEZE' you." (21)

Forgiveness can be part of our spiritual healing.

However, it may take time and a lot of spiritual grief work to accomplish such a difficult task. How do you forgive someone who has hurt you? Acts of betrayal may be the most painful. Many have asked, "Can I forgive a perpetrator if they have not repented?" "Can I forgive without hearing the words 'I am sorry'?"

"The reality of the situation is that no amount of talking, no analysis of why the betrayal occurred will completely do away with the hurt. No penalty can be handed down that will satisfactorily pay off the debt. No matter how cruelly you've been treated, the power to forgive does not lie within the person who hurt you...the blocks to forgiveness are ultimately within you. Forgiveness can stop the cycle of hurt." (21) (permission to quote Dr. Paul W. Coleman)

"It's difficult to recognize the personal benefits of forgiving another person who has intentionally hurt us. When our wounds are deep and our scars permanent, offering forgiveness to an unrepentant offender may seem impossible. Under such circumstance the old "eye for an eye" approach is a tempting solution to personally extract our 'deserved' pound of flesh. Unfortunately substituting another's pain for our own brings no permanent resolution or true healing. Substitution provides revenge while resolution through forgiveness allows healing to take place regardless of the location or attitude of the offender.

The following false beliefs and biases can limit our ability to forgive someone who has betrayed us:
1. Forgiving lets the perpetrator get away with some thing.
2. Forgiveness is a sign of personal weakness.
3. Forgiving will cause the abuse to occur again.

4. Not forgiving helps punish the perpetrator.

5. The perpetrator must repent or apologize before I can forgive.

"It has taken years for me to understand how he could have abused me when I was such a small child. I've finally come to feel sorry for him, let go of the hate, and start to forgive."

A forty-year-old woman revealed that, as a young girl, she had experienced sexual abuse by her father. He died before she became an adult. In an attempt to help her let go and forgive her father, Dennis used a counseling aid that utilizes visualization and guided imagery to help her heal.

She pictured herself with a large group of people who loved her. The Savior was also present and expressed his love and acceptance of her. When she was ready, she could open a door where her father was. When she decided to open the door and saw her father, she screamed, yelled and confronted him. Through her tears she realized that he, too, had been abused and in this safe environment began to feel compassion toward him. She was ultimately able to offer him forgiveness and later claimed her depression was lifted.

The following member was able to forgive an unfaithful spouse:

"My spouse has been unfaithful. After our divorce he remarried and divorced again. We have now decided to try and to put our temple marriage back together. It's been so hard to trust and forgive. However, I feel I need to try."

How do you forgive the man who robbed, raped or murdered your loved one?

"My daughter was raped and murdered. It has been

seven years. I will never forget or get over it. However, I am trying to forgive."

Although very difficult, the Lord asks that we forgive ourselves and others: "...ye ought to forgive one another;...it is required to forgive all men." (D&C 64:8-11 and Matt. 18:35)

The following tools have proven helpful to those attempting to offer forgiveness:

1. Write a letter to the offender.

2. Keep a journal of your feelings and memories.

3. Visualize and confront the offender (by imagining him sitting in an empty chair or through guided imagery).

"Forgiveness is an ongoing process. It is a gift you give yourself. Christ offered us forgiveness...before we ever needed or asked for it." (22 5/1/99 p.15)

The Lord has said that "Vengeance is mine, I will repay." (Mormon 3:15) Satan is the author of un-forgiveness. (2 Corin. 2:10-11)

OPPOSITION

The Lord explains, "For it must needs be, that there is opposition in all things...righteousness...wickedness, holiness...misery...good...bad..." (2 Nephi 2:11)

He has also told us "...and they taste the bitter, that they may know to prize the good..." (Moses 6:55-56) "Only the soul that knows the mighty pain can know the mighty rapture." (3)

OMNIPOTENCE

God not only weeps with us as we experience pain, he also loves and comforts us through His power. We must remember His omnipotence even when the answer to our prayer is "no" or the comfort comes in a different way than we expected.

PERSONAL REVELATION/ IMPRESSIONS/ VISIONS
(See more in Ch. 10.)

Personal revelation and impressions can bring healing and comfort. God has given us the gift of the Holy Ghost, one of the most powerful spiritual tools available.

"And though the Lord give you the bread of adversity, and the water of affliction, yet shall not thy teachers be removed into a corner any more, but thine eyes shall see thy teachers: And thine ears shall hear a word behind thee, saying, This is the way, walk ye in it, when ye turn to the right hand, and when ye turn to the left." (Isa. 30:20-21)

Those facing adversities can receive spiritual healing through personal revelation which can come from impressions, dreams and visions.

I wrote the following experience in my journal:

"I received some spiritual impressions and insight today. I was doing the laundry, of all things. I was feeling confused about life and God's intervention in it. I had just talked to several women whose husbands had left them and their families. As I listened to their pain, I wondered how God could stand to watch their suffering and not cause a great miracle and take away all of their pain. Why didn't he intervene and change their situations? The words that came to me were simple. I had heard them a hundred times before. But now the power of the spirit overwhelmed me. What I heard in my heart was this: 'The Lord, God, knows the end from the beginning.'" (Isaiah

46:10, 1 Nephi 9:6)

This experience rang true to me because for several years I facilitated bereavement groups at a community hospital. The neonatal loss group provided support and direction for parents who experienced a miscarriage, stillbirth, or ectopic pregnancy. When I first started working with this group, I hurt almost as deeply as my clients. Their experiences caused me to remember and mourn my own losses. I wondered how I could help them resolve or get through their intense grief. With time I would see them heal, get pregnant or adopt beautiful babies. After watching over a hundred families each year journey from despair to happiness, I stopped hurting so much. I could now see or imagine the "end from the beginning". I knew with time, grief work, and prayer they could work through most of their grief. For most, having another baby did not cause them to forget the one they had lost. However, parents who lose a baby can eventually reconcile their grief and feel joy and happiness again.

God knows that many are suffering unfairly, often at the hands of others. Remember, death, disease, and pain are all part of the plan we accepted when we agreed to earth life. God generally does not take away the agency of spouses or others who cause us harm. Fortunately, He has not left us alone. He has provided the Holy Ghost to comfort us.

Visions, like impressions, have been a source of knowledge and comfort for many. A stake Relief Society president came to LDS Family Services because she was feeling serious conflict in her life. Initially it seemed that she was simply overly involved in too many worthwhile projects in addition to her own busy calling and family. She gained insight as she identified self-defeating behaviors in her life and was soon able to say "no" without fear of rejection, set some priorities, and cut back on some duties. Throughout the therapy, however, she didn't feel she was receiving the peace she had desired. One day as she was praying she had a vision. She saw herself as a little girl sitting on a stool in the kitchen with her feet dangling in the air. Her mother was accusing her of not telling the truth. She had just told her mother that her brother had been sexually abusing her. Her mother told her that her brother would never do "that". Her vision of this past painful experience opened up new opportunities to help her. Her recollection was followed by understanding and healing as she was finally able to deal with the true source of her pain and insecurities. Following her insight, she was able to acknowledge the pain, work through the issues and ultimately let it go.

Dennis and I had impressions that caused us to believe that we might prematurely lose our fourteen-year-old disabled son, Cameron. I often feared he would die from an accident that I hadn't protected him from. He regularly fell off his tricycle and even with his helmet on and seemed vulnerable. However, I didn't anticipate that he would slip away in his sleep in a close observation room with bright lights, Dennis and a nurse at his side.

Two years after Cameron's death, both of us were surprised how much we still missed and mourned for him. One day as I was feeling particularly sad and discouraged, I cried out in prayer, "How long will it hurt so much? Why does the pain keep coming back?" Then I heard a still small voice in my heart and mind that directed me to read in the Bible. I turned to Jeremiah chapter thirty one, "A strange place to read," I thought. I knew I hadn't read much from there before. When I got to verses fifteen through seventeen my heart leaped. I felt the Lord was trying to comfort me, along with all those who have or ever will lose a loved one!

"Thus saith the Lord; A voice was heard in Ramah,

lamentation and bitter weeping; Rahel weeping for her children refused to be comforted for her children, because they were not. Thus saith the Lord; Refrain thy voice from weeping, and thine eyes from tears: for thy work shall be rewarded, saith the Lord; and they shall come again.... And there is hope in thine end saith the Lord, that thy children shall come again..." (Jeremiah 30:15-17)

This scripture hit me with great force and power. I realized later that this counsel was given to mothers who were mourning for their children that King Herod had ordered killed. (Matthew 3:17-18) These inspired words gave me increased faith and the strength I needed to endure the wait! (Isa. 40:31; D&C 98: 2-3)

Impressions and revelations have blessed many during adversity. Some are surprised by the answers they have received.

"I have tried for many years to keep my temple marriage intact. I have received comfort from the spirit and many impressions on how to do this. Even after my husband had left us and was excommunicated, I believed we would work things out and stay together. I was shocked after much fasting and prayer when I received an impression to file for divorce."

Another woman, surprised by the answer she received said:

"My husband had been unfaithful, divorced me, remarried, and divorced again. I was shocked when I received a answer after much fasting and prayer to give him another chance and put our temple marriage back together."

An unwed mother writes:

"As much as I want to keep my baby, I received a strong impression that if I really love and care about him, I should place him for adoption with LDS Family Services so he could be sealed to both a mother and a father."

FAITH

Having faith and hope does not mean things will always come out how we'd like. It does mean we must trust the Lord to comfort and help us through. Remember the Kosovo social worker we spoke of previously who explained that the reason his people wanted to return to their destroyed homes and land was because the "hope in their hearts could not be destroyed"? "For we are saved by hope: but hope that is seen is not hope: for what a man seeth, why doth he yet hope for?" (Romans 8:24) The Lord has told us to keep the commandments so our faith won't fail. (D&C 136:42) One's faith can be a healing tool for grief recovery:

"The only way to meet affliction is to pass through it solemnly, slowly, with humility and faith, as the Israelites passed through the Red sea. Then its very waves of misery will divide, and become to us a wall, on the right side and on the left, until the gulf narrows before our eyes, and we will land safe on the opposite shore." (23)

However, we have been told that not all have faith (D&C 88: 118) and that faith is a gift. (1 Cor. 12:9) We all have different gifts and we are not to judge the faithless. (Rom. 14:1-5)

Dennis and I have friends who are pilots. They often enjoy a clear sky when they fly above the clouds, even though down below we might be buried under a blanket of dark clouds. Sometimes our lives are like that—all we can see is the darkness. "For now I see through a glass darkly;..." (1 Cor. 13:12) However, the reality is, the sun is always shining. The "SON" is also always shining for us, even when we find ourselves in the black pit of despair. (24)

We can have faith and tap into spiritual tools to know his power and see clearer. "But then face to face...shall I know even as also I am known." (I Cor. 13:12) We must "Walk by Faith" (2 Cor. 5: 7), and faith can purify our hearts. (Acts 15:9) The definition of faith according to the Kings James Bible Dictionary is: "Faith is to hope for things which are not seen, but are true."

The Bible tells us, "Now faith is the substance of things hoped for, the evidence of things not seen" (Hebrews 11:1), and that we won't receive a witness until after the trial of our faith. (Ether 12: 6) The Lord has said, "I will try the faith of my people". (3 Nephi 26:11), and that Christ is the author of faith. (Moroni 6:4)

The brother of Jared displayed great faith. He progressed from faith, asking the Lord to touch the stones that they might have light, to pure, absolute knowledge, and ultimately he saw HIM! Our faith may not be as complete as the brother of Jared; however, his example can increase our faith.

The parable of the mustard seed provides insight on how we can nurture our faith. The mustard seed is one of the smallest seeds, yet if nourished it can grow into a large tree. After a loss some of us may have to start over again by replanting a tiny seed of hope. We can let our desire for faith work in us as we nourish our little seed day by day and exercise faith that it will grow. (Alma 32)

We may rediscover that there is a God who will comfort us and help us through our tragedies. "If ye have faith as a grain of mustard seed, nothing shall be impossible to you." (Matt. 17:20) "If ye have enough faith, God will give you what ye ask for." (1 Nephi 7:12) This scripture may confuse those who don't get their prayers answered immediately or the way they'd hoped for. However, it has given others the hope and strength to keep asking. Wendy Ulrich Ph.D., a friend and AMCAP (Association of Mormon Counselors and Psychotherapists) colleague, discussed the following paradoxes: 1. Knowledge without certainty. It is important to accept the necessity of faith or, as David Tracy, says: "It is good enough knowledge." (26) We can have peace amid uncertainty. 2. Presence in absence. We can believe and feel the spiritual presence of God in his physical absence. We can practice this privately or through our church service, prayer and temple worship. (25) In this discussion of faith we need to remember that having faith does not preclude us from also experiencing grief.

SERVICE

Service can be a powerful spiritual tool that offers relief from our grief. It helps us forget our problems as we discover that there are others suffering around us who could use our help, acceptance and understanding.

Dennis found while working on the hospital psychiatric unit that those patients who recovered the quickest were those able to reach out and help another patient. "Those who bring sunshine to others cannot keep it from themselves." (Sir James Barrie) (12 p.90)

We often forget the power of giving and living the gospel. It sometimes becomes so routine we take for granted how blessed we are to have these healing tools in our lives. Offering service or becoming a servant often humbles us. "Be thou humble; and the Lord...shall lead thee and...answer thy prayers." (D&C 112:10)

CHURCH ATTENDANCE

Many of us will find it difficult to attend church during

and after a crisis. The songs and lessons that once offered comfort to us now may remind us of our loss. Cameron was able to pass the sacrament with the use of a special metal tray attached to the arm of his electric wheelchair. We loved watching him do this. For a long time after his death it was very difficult to watch the sacrament being passed without his being there.

"It's so hard to sit on the pew without my wife next to me."

"I felt like I was under glass, like everyone was staring at me, wondering how I was doing. The lessons seemed so trite compared to what I was facing."

There are many who find increased peace and comfort at church following a crisis.

A friend said after her adversity:

"I am just loving going to church, Sunday School, Relief Society, etc.! I am soaking up every word. I am craving the Spirit right now."

Eventually most of us can return to church as we redefine and accept our "new normal." The peace, comfort and fellowship of worship can, with time, bring lasting happiness and comfort.

SACRAMENT BLESSINGS

Do we only find God in times of peace, happiness and abundance? Do we miss out on growing experiences and God's love looking for it only in times of smooth sailing? Do we believe God loves us unconditionally? Are we only blessed when things are going well? While working with members during loss, some have asked if they are "still blessed." It is a common phrase we hear often during fast and testimony meetings.

When someone says, "I am blessed," what does that mean? Does it mean we have no problems in our lives, or that we are just focusing on the good things in our lives? If we are having a lot of adversity in our life, can we still be "blessed"? When we ask God to bless us, we may be seeking something specific or asking for protection. However, aren't we actually seeking His Spirit to be with us? The sacrament prayer found in D&C 20:77, 79, confirms this. "...always remember him and keep his commandments...that they may always have his Spirit to be with them." We can have His spirit with us even during adversity.

TEMPLES

Elder Dallin Oaks teaches:
"One of the purposes of building a temple is to present to the Lord a house in which He can reveal Himself and His mysteries to His faithful children." (22 10/31/92 p.11)

Many have found the temple to be a safe and peaceful refuge during adversity. Three months after Cameron's death, Dennis performed his temple work. It was a very small company with only one row of women and two rows of men. Dennis sat on the second row of the men's side. I kept feeling like someone was sitting behind me. I looked back; however, the whole back of the room was empty. The feeling became so intense that I came to believe Cameron must be sitting behind me! I couldn't see him, I just felt his presence. It was confusing to me, because I thought, "If he could come and watch his ordinance for himself, why would he sit on the women's side?" Was it just my imagination, or wishful thinking? After the ceremony, I asked Dennis if he thought it was possible for Cameron's spirit to be present? He said, "I believe so, and he seemed to be sitting right behind you!" This confirmed our impressions and brought both of us comfort and spiritual healing. However, this post-death impression was never repeated and we know many wonderful members who hoped for a similar impression, vision, or revelation that did not come.

One of my childhood friends recently confided in me:
"I have wanted to feel the presence of my deceased son in the temple. It seems odd that others tell me they feel him there and I do not."

We don't understand all of the workings of the spirit in the temple. There may be many factors involved in explaining why someone does or does not receive a particular spiritual gift. (See chp.10 p.174)

MYSTERIES

Many of our spiritual frustrations don't end with, "Okay Lord, now I understand, I see why these terrible things are happening to me." Rather, we must file many things away as a mystery, something we just can't understand. Nephi said, "God loveth his children; Nevertheless, I do not know the meaning of all things." (I Nephi 11:17)

Part of faith is knowing there are mysteries. Our natural eyes cannot see and understand all. The Greek term "mystery" means "to close the eyes or to close the mouth."

The Lord sent Elijah to hide in the Kerith Ravine. He said that Elijah would drink from the brook and the ravens would feed him. (1 Kings 17) It must have been a mystery to Elijah when the brook dried up.

The word "mystery" appears in the New Testament twenty four times. Paul speaks of "the mysteries of God" in 1 Cor. 4:1. "The mysteries of God's will" is found in Ephesians 1:9. "The mystery of Christ's presence within human beings" is in Cor. 1:27.

Although there are many mysteries, we are blessed as members of Christ's church to have the restored Gospel which reveals more spiritual knowledge than all other Christian doctrines combined.

Elder Oaks teaches:

"The Melchizedek Priesthood gives us access to the mysteries of God...through this priesthood we receive the gift of the Holy Ghost, by which we are taught the things of God..." (22 10/31/92 p.11)

PRIESTHOOD / PRAYER / FASTING / SCRIPTURES

These spiritual tools are listed last because most members are aware of them and use them regularly. However, as members of the church we often take them for granted, not fully comprehending their power to comfort and heal us spiritually. We need God's power in our lives to heal from adversity.

"Who shall separate us from the love of Christ? Shall tribulation, or distress, or persecution, or famine, or nakedness, or peril, or sword?...Nay in all these things we are more than conquerors through him that loved us. For I am persuaded, that neither death, nor life, nor angels, nor principalities, nor powers, nor things present, nor things to come, nor height, nor depth, nor any other creature, shall be able to separate us from the love of God..." (Romans 8:35, 37-39)

Do we pray as fervently during good times as we do during our adversity? Even the Savior seemed to turn to God more fervently during his agony and suffering, "Being in agony he prayed more earnestly." (Luke 22:44)

We can reach the Lord through praying, fasting, priesthood blessings, attending church, the temple and reading scriptures. However, many struggling individuals cannot initially turn to these tools during their crises. Some individuals have reluctantly shared:

"It is so difficult to pray to a God who allowed this to happen to my family."

It's important for us to keep trying and not give up. Remember that eventually most will be able to return to their faith and reach out to God again. It will then be possible for us to tap into the power of the Holy Ghost, who is literally referred to as *The Comforter*.

One member described it well when she wrote:

"I have prayed, fasted, attended the temple and received a priesthood blessing in hopes of being relieved of my adversity. However, my adversity still remains. Now I pray, fast, attend the temple and receive blessings to help me ENDURE my adversity."

HOW DO WE ENDURE TO THE END?

Enduring to the end may mean a variety of things to each of us. Sometimes accepting our adversity is the first step to enduring and healing. I have grown to admire those I work with in hospice. Many suffer day in and day out, week after week, month after month, wondering when death will bring relief. It is hard on those suffering, and those caregivers watching, loving and often providing backbreaking care.

Enduring is a principle of the gospel. Many righteous people have had to endure suffering. Ten of Christ's twelve disciples were executed. Stephen was stoned. Joseph Smith, Job and David had to endure adversity and felt forsaken. Even as Christ suffered on the cross, he asked his Father, "Why hast thou forsaken me?" (Matt. 27:46) Many people suffering have asked that same question. It is helpful to look to Christ as our example; he too, had to experience earthly pain and suffering of His own free will:

"Though he were a son, yet learned he obedience by the things which he suffered, and being made perfect, he became the author of eternal salvation unto all them that obeyed him." (Hebrews 5:8)

The Prophet Joseph Smith also called out to the Lord in Liberty Jail for relief from his suffering:

"Oh God, where art thou?... Yea, O Lord, how long shall they suffer these wrongs and unlawful oppressions, before thine heart shall be softened toward them, and...[thou] be moved with compassion towards them?" (D&C 121:1,3)

He was told in verse seven "My son, peace be unto thy soul; thine adversity and thine afflictions shall be but a small moment." The Lord provided support as he continued to discuss Joseph's afflictions. However, he never removed them.

"If thou art called to pass through tribulation...If thou art accused with all manner of false accusations;...and thou be dragged to prison,...and the sentence of death passed upon thee;...if fierce winds become thine enemy; if the heavens gather blackness, and all the elements combine to hedge up the way; and above all, if the very jaws of hell shall gape open the mouth wide after thee, know thou, my son, that all these things shall give thee experience, and shall be for thy good. The Son of Man hath descended below them all. Art thou greater than He?...fear not what man can do, for God shall be with you forever and ever." (D&C Section 122, verses 5–9)

Enduring often means not giving up in the face of serious challenges and adversity. "Press forward with a brightness of hope." (2 Nephi 31:20)

Elder Maxwell teaches:

"When in situations of stress we wonder if there is any more in us to give, we can be comforted to know that God, who knows our capability perfectly, placed us here to succeed. No one was foreordained to fail or to be wicked. When we have been weighed and found wanting, let us remember that we were measured before and found equal to our tasks; and, therefore, let us continue, but with a more determined discipleship..." (11) "Patience is not to be mistaken for indifference. It is to care very much, but to be willing, nevertheless, to submit both to the Lord and to what the scriptures call the 'process of time.'" (11)

Orson F. Whitney taught:

"No pain that we suffer, no trial that we experience is wasted. It ministers to our education, to the development of such qualities as patience, faith, fortitude and humility. All that we suffer and all that we ENDURE, especially when we ENDURE it patiently, builds up our character, purifies our hearts, expands our souls, and makes us more tender and charitable, more worthy to be called the children of God." (27 p. 98)

The scriptures encourage us to "endure afflictions." (2 Tim. 4:5) "We must endure tribulation." (Acts 14: 22) "Behold we count them happy which endure." (James 5:11) "Wherefore, if ye shall be obedient to the commandment, and endure to the end, ye shall be saved at the last day." (1 Nephi 22:31) "Be patient in afflictions, for thou shalt have many; but endure them, for, lo, I am with thee, even unto the end of thy days." (D&C 24:8) "Endure it well, God shall exalt thee..." (D&C 121:8.) "Has the Lord forgotten you? No, he has engraven you on his hands." (1 Nephi 21:14-16)

God loves us and allows us to experience joy and pain. He is acquainted with grief. (Isaiah 53:3-5) He can help us "remember our pain no more." (Alma 36:19) With faith, prayer, study and the other spiritual tools mentioned, we can find peace and come to understand and accept how God operates in our world. With time, patience and grief work we can come to understand that grief is a process; recovery or adaptation is a choice; and resolution is a journey rather than a destination.

SECTION III :

OTHER CONSIDERATIONS FOR ENDURING LOSS

Chapters 10-13

CHAPTER 10

DEATH AND SPIRITUALITY

The death of a loved one can be a significant loss for many. Dennis and I have shared throughout this book stories of the many loved ones that have died within our family. We felt we dealt with them pretty well until our son Cameron died, then we were devastated.

I see a variety of reactions to death as I am working with older, terminally ill people in hospice. There are many ready and wanting death. Many of their families feel they have led a full life and are ready to let them go. There are many factors that determine how we will cope. (See figure #2.)

"Death is not extinguishing the light; it is putting out the lamp because the dawn has come." (1 p.12)

We discussed spiritual healing during adversity in the last chapter. After the death of a loved one, some have received additional spiritual healing from personal impressions, visions, dreams, visitations, Near-Death-Experiences (NDE), or At-Death Experiences (ADE). These experiences may also serve as death preparations.

We would like to share some of the comforting experiences and spiritual impressions that helped our family deal with the death of our disabled son, Cameron. Cameron wrote the following poem for a school project six months before his death.

If I Had a Wish

If I had a wish I would wish that I could walk!
I would run and play and all the girls would like me.
See it's hard to be different in some ways.
Like you can't do your homework without someone
helping you.
Sports would be fun to do, and I would play basketball.
And I wouldn't miss standing in my prone stander if I
could walk.
In some ways not walking is good luck because you get to
drive early! (My wheelchair) and you don't even have to
have a license.
You also can have a computer all to yourself.
My wish will come true—in the "Next Life!" (2 p. 141-2)

The day Cameron died, his Special Education teacher in Texas remembered the poem he had written earlier about his wishes. She had trouble sleeping and early that morning she got up and wrote the following poem:

"Written in response to the death of Cameron Ashton and his private wish for his Next Life."

THE WISH

I felt the breath of death today. It brushed against my cheek. And left me most unconscious, taking thought and words to speak. It left me feeling empty, and lost within myself. It crept about my being like a mouse on pantry shelf. I wandered aimless through the day and half the lonely night, but came a "Great Awakening" at break of morning light, I saw a child in field of green with yellow flowers round. He was moving swiftly through the grass on limbs so strong and sound. His laughter rang within my ear as clear as Sunday's bell. His smile did light the broad blue sky and caused the clouds to swell. I watched as one who's privileged eyes had glimpsed through Heaven's door, and just as quickly saw it close, revealing nothing more. Then as a wave upon a shore, washes it so clean. My torched mind was cleared to see that this was not a dream. The sorrow felt inside my heart belonged to only me. For how could I be sad for one who's now so free? I swept away a tear that trickled down my cheek. And rose to meet the bright new day that God had given me. I felt witness to a sacred time, not really meant to me. For how often does God grant a wish and allow someone to see!? (2 p.145-6)

We didn't know her well and she was initially hesitant to share her poem with us. It wasn't until after Cameron's funeral that she decided to shared her spiritual impressions with us. After Cameron's funeral she went home and returned with the poem. She is not a member of the church. She mentioned several times during our discussion that she had never been touched spiritually so profoundly by any student during her fifteen years of teaching. Her poem brought us personal comfort.

Cameron talked of death and his next life often. The following is his testimony from a pre-recorded video six weeks before his death. While Dennis was taping, he had the impression that what Cameron was saying was deeply significant, more than the typical family video session. It took Cameron more than fourteen minutes to meticulously share his impressions, which, after being typed—doubled spaced—took up less than one page. This is the conclusion of his recording. It's the only recorded testimony we have from him:

"I really feel that I can walk in the next life, and that I can talk better. And that I will live forever in the next life after this and that I will see God again. And I get to see my Grandma and Grandpa who died a couple of years ago, again. And you can too someday. I guess I don't have to say anymore. And this is Cameron signing off."

Soon after Cameron's death I was walking through the "sand hills" to which I had often escaped to as a teenager. I was crying, praying, and mourning, "Why did he have to die? Where is he? I miss him so much! Why, Why, Why?" I then heard the following words as thoughts and impressions. They may have been simple, logical thoughts that anyone could have said to me. However, when these thoughts and impressions came to my mind through the spirit, I felt truth and power in the words: First, I was released from my calling as the caregiver of a disabled child. Second, Cameron still existed and was doing something important. Third, I too, still had an earthly purpose or mission that needed to be completed. I made the decision that morning to make the best of my deep grief and sadness, and to find out what the rest of my earthly mission entailed. Of course, I did not know then how hard and long the journey ahead would be.

HEALING DREAMS

Most of us dream about one and one-half hours each night. (3 pg. 72) Dreams often have elements from our past, present and sometimes our futures. Although we might not remember all that we dream, dreams can bring us significant insight. The scriptures contain accounts of individuals being guided by theirs or others' dreams. One of the most familiar accounts is when Joseph is warned in a dream to flee from King Herod with Mary and baby Jesus. (Matt. 2:13)

A mother in my bereavement group shared the following dream she had about her seven-year-old prior to his death: She and her seven-year-old were in a large crowd and became separated. She became very emotional and woke up crying because she had actually allowed him to go and didn't try to find him. The dream left her distraught and concerned. She wondered what the dream meant. Her son had also recently asked her what it was like to die. She remembers telling him that someone he knew would meet him. (See p. 171 where his great-grandpa meets him.) This was a healthy boy who suddenly became ill and died twenty four hours later from a virus. Before he died his mother thought she heard the words, "Mommy, please stop calling me back, I want to live with Jesus." She then realized, "I had been willing him in my mind to fight and come back to me."

My own mother was only fourteen when her father died. She recalls waking up from a very real dream about his death. She cried and mourned his loss; later that morning when she was told he actually had died, she felt somehow better prepared by the dream.

I didn't remember my mother's dream until long after I had experienced my own dream about Cameron's death. One week before Cam's surgery I dreamed his surgery was over and the doctors said they needed to talk to me. They told me he was having trouble breathing and would have to be on life support and would not be able to live without it. The doctors recommended the removal of life support, however, it was my decision. I went into his room and watched the cardiac monitor move with each thump of his heart. I knew that if I told them to turn off the ventilator, the line on the heart monitor would soon go straight. I thought about my choice for a while. Finally I ran out of the room crying; I could not tell them to unplug my child's life! I wanted him alive! The dream was so real I woke up sobbing. I felt very sad and afraid! I shared my dream with my mother and later with Dennis. He related similar feelings and death preparation experiences that had caused him to worry about Cameron also.

The night before his surgery, at family home evening, we shared the dream with Cameron. We didn't want to frighten him. He had just turned fourteen. We wanted him to know how much we loved him and how we would miss him. I told him if something did go wrong and he actually died, would he please try to somehow let me know he was okay and happy in the spirit world. He nodded yes. As I looked at his big, tearful brown eyes, I realized this could be a hard promise to keep. I then told him if he couldn't return and tell me (visitation), I would try to just have enough faith to know that he was well. He obediently agreed like he usually did when we made requests of him. Although we had this open discussion during family night, none of us really believed it would happen.

We did not think about the dream or family discussion until several days after his death when my mother reminded us. Remembering the dream brought comfort mixed with guilt, "Why didn't we cancel his surgery?" "Was the dream a warning?" However, with time we chose to believe the dream was a glimpse into the future, becoming an important death preparation that brought us comfort.

After-death dreams can offer comfort as well. In one dream, I was crying and mourning Cameron's death. In the middle of the dream I was impressed to get up and read the words to the hymn #117, *Come Unto Jesus*. I woke myself from the dream and went to read the words. The following words brought peace and comfort, "Oh know ye not that angels are near you from brightest mansions above?"

VISIONS

Some feel it is hard to tell the difference between a dream and a vision. Others say a vision is real and we are awake and see what is happening, whereas in dreams we know we are sleeping. Visions may occur in the day or at night. The Bible mentions "night visions." (1 Daniel 2:19)

My mother remembers, as a fourteen-year-old girl, how sad her own mother was when her husband died of cancer. Eight months later she followed him to the grave after a car accident. Although it was hard on my mother to lose both of her parents so close together, she felt some relief because she believed her mother was relieved of her grief and was now with her husband. One of her brothers, a patriarch, said later that he saw both parents together in a vision. This brought much comfort to the ten children they had left behind.

The wonderful vision and revelation (D&C 138) received by Joseph F. Smith concerning the redemption of the dead came following the death of his adult child. President Smith agonized for nine months following his son's death. He wondered why he remained alive in his eighties, while his gifted, worthy son in his forties was gone. He felt grief, and through his loss sought greater understanding. President Smith's grief, prayer, and searching allowed him to receive many comforting doctrinal truths. He died soon after the recording of his vision that later was accepted as revelation and canonized as section 138 of the Doctrine and Covenants.

Joseph Smith had a vision where he saw the gate and beautiful streets of the Celestial Kingdom. He writes, "Whether in the body or out I cannot tell." (D&C 137:1) He was surprised to see his brother, Alvin, there. He then received the revelation explaining how it was possible that his deceased brother was there even though he hadn't had the opportunity to hear or receive the gospel and be baptized. "...All who have died without a knowledge of this gospel, who would have received it if they had been permitted to tarry, shall be heirs of the celestial kingdom of God...." (D&C 137:7)

A father in my bereavement group shared the following vision: He was lying by his critically ill young son in the ICU unit. Although the life support seemed to still be working, this dad felt that his son's spirit had already left his body. As he was meditating about how he would deal with his son's death, he saw his son's spirit in the hospital hallway walking with his deceased great-grandfather! Soon after this vision, the doctors came and told him that although his son appeared to be alive, there was no brain activity, and that the life support would be removed. In all our years of counseling we have never seen a father accept the death of a child so peacefully. We feel the vision of his son and deceased grandfather together is what helped him accept his son's death.

Many enduring adversity wish they could have a comforting vision, but do not. (See p. 173) Sister See desired a vision or visit from her deceased thirteen-year-old. When it didn't happen, she turned to the scriptures for comfort. D&C: 24:4 jumped out at her as an answer to her plea:

"Murmur not because of the things which thou hast not seen, for they are withheld from thee and from the world, which is wisdom in me in a time to come." (4 Oct. 1998)

VISITATIONS

A visitation is the act of being visited by a deceased person. Although many visitations seem to occur as dreams, some occur while the person is awake and during daylight hours.

One such visitation occurred to a woman seated at her sewing machine. Her mother who had been dead for sometime came with an important message for her. She said, "Daughter, you don't know what it has cost me to come to you." (5 p. 84) Many of us have wondered, "What is the cost, and why do some deceased spirits visit while others do not?" Another similar account was prompted by a deceased individual's strong desire to have her temple ordinances done. She firmly said, "You are the only one I have to depend on... Don't fail in this." (5 p. 86)

One day in a counseling session with Dennis, a widower described in detail a visit from his deceased wife. It concerned him very much because she had encouraged him to marry a certain woman that they both knew. She felt that he needed someone to help take care of their children. He wasn't really sure he was ready to marry, or if he wanted to marry this particular woman!

In 1993 approximately sixty six percent of widows experienced apparitions after their husbands died (6). Of course, some professionals feel these are acute grief hallucinations; however, one interesting account disproving intense grief as the cause is of a man's wife visiting him eighteen years after her death. (7 p. 65) His acute grief would no longer be present, decreasing any possibility of a stress-related hallucination.

A comforting experience occurred when a deceased mother appeared to her grieving daughter and said, "I was allowed to come and tell you not to be worried about me. I don't suffer anymore and I am very happy" (7 p. 44) (She died of cancer). She made it clear that she had to have permission to come.

A reported visitation in Cokeville, Wyoming received national news coverage. Elementary school children who were being held hostage at gunpoint described how they were warned about a bomb that was about to explode in their class-room. They claimed individuals dressed in white standing in the air told them where to go and how to seek safety. There was more than one account and all the children lived after the bomb exploded to tell their stories. Following the event some of the children were shown pictures of dead relatives they hadn't personally known. Some were recognized as the individuals in white who had helped them. (8) It seems that on occasion departed loved ones may be allowed to return to offer comfort, warn, or share important messages.

In a 1993 report, seventy-five percent of parents surveyed who had lost children claimed they had an apparition involving their child. (6) On the other hand, some survivors of Near-Death Experiences report that they asked while in the spirit world for permission to communicate with the living and were denied the privilege.

NO VISITATION

After Cameron died, Dennis and especially myself, thought he would return and give us a message. When he did not it was confusing and disappointing. We began to question our worthiness, which we have learned is a common concern:

"There are many of our Latter-day Saint mothers who have mourned the loss of their little children, and many mothers have felt that they themselves had committed some great sin, else their little ones would not be taken from them. Now, to such mothers let me say, do not accuse the Lord of taking your little ones from you, nor feel that you have committed any great sin, that those little ones are taken from you, because the Lord loves little children and he will not treat them unkindly, nor without mercy, for through the blood of his atonement they shall come forth in the morning of the resurrection with his saints, and they shall be glorified according to the works they would have accomplished in the earth had they lived." (9)

As time went on, Dennis and I decided to take a different view of why Cameron didn't appear to us after his death. We thought possibly he shouldn't or couldn't appear to us; or as described previously, the "cost" was too high. We tried to think positively; maybe Cameron was honoring his covenants or priesthood duty by not appearing to us.

We also looked to the scripture, "Blessed are they that have not seen, and yet have believed." (John 20:29) We have tried to believe that we must simply have faith.

An Amalekite in the Book of Mormon asked why Aaron was allowed to see an angel. "Why do not angels appear unto us? Behold are not this people as good as thy people?" (Alma 21:5) Many members have wondered the same, questioning their worthiness.

Louis E. LaGrand lists why he feels mourners do not have contact experiences with their deceased loved one.

1. They do not possibly need one.
2. They cannot believe it would occur.
3. Their fear causes repression or suppression of an event.
4. They may have negative states that preclude any positive experience; anger, pessimism, or any negative emotion.
5. Most important, I feel, is the teaching of Paul in Corinthians (Cor. 12:8-11) concerning individual spiritual gifts; we all have different gifts, teaching, preaching, prophecy, recognizing angels/spirits etc. (10) Moroni 10: 9-17 also lists the gifts of knowledge, faith, healing, tongues, working miracles, and the beholding of angels and spirits. Some of us apparently are not to receive the gift of "beholding angles and spirits." (10)

President W. Woodruff discusses the issue:

"One of the Apostles said to me years ago, "Brother Woodruff, I have prayed for a long time for the Lord to send the administration of an angel to me. I have had a great desire for this, but I have never had my prayers answered." I said to him that if he were to pray a thousand years to the God of Israel for that gift it would not be granted, unless the Lord had a motive in sending an angel to him. I told him that the Lord never did nor never will send an angel to anybody merely to gratify the desire of the individuals to see an angel. If the Lord sends an angel to anyone, He sends him to perform a work that cannot be performed only by the administration of an angel." (11 p. 63)

NEAR-DEATH EXPERIENCES (NDE)

Many people find spiritual comfort from reading accounts of Near-Death Experiences. The Apostle Paul describes an out-of-body experience in 2 Cor. 12:2-4. More than eight million people have reported having Near-Death Experiences. (6)

Some reports of NDE's occur following an illness or accident where individuals lose consciousness, or where their heart has stopped beating, requiring resuscitation efforts. They may find themselves traveling outside their body. Some report traveling down a tunnel with vibrating sounds. Others view their physical body from above and report the details of their own resuscitation. Many see a light or spirit being. Some are greeted by deceased relatives. They often describe a brightness and beauty beyond anything earthly. Most profoundly they feel an unconditional, overpowering love and acceptance. The importance of love for fellow man is reinforced. Many visually experience a review of their lives. Often the life events reviewed and reinforced that are of greatest importance are those where they showed kindness and love to others. Personal accomplishments did not seem most significant. It wasn't the honors or praise of men. Rather, it was the love and charity they showed to other human beings. Most Near Death Experiences seem to also emphasize the importance of obtaining wisdom and knowledge while on the earth. One of my clients wrote her own NDE for me. It fits the pattern that so many others have described:

"During a difficult childbirth, I went into shock and had an emergency C-section. I was on the operating table for three hours.

"I was exhausted and things seemed to get smaller, softer, and gently fade away. I heard a strange buzzing noise. The next thing I remember is looking down and seeing myself in the operating room. I heard the nurse say that my heart and the baby's heart were slowing down. This neither surprised or upset me. I watched all this like I was just a spectator.

"It is so hard to describe all the events that happened next. No words are applicable to the sights and sounds that I encountered. At some point I was inside a dark tunnel. I am very nearsighted, but while going through this experience, my eyesight was perfect. I saw everything around me simultaneously, yet individually. I don't remember looking at what kind of body I had because I still felt like myself and all this seemed normal. I didn't realize I was dying. On both sides of me was something similar to being in outer space. Far down the tunnel I could see an indescribable brilliant white light. From both sides of the tunnel I could hear beautiful music with voices singing, but not in English. I could understand it and the sounds were like nothing I'd ever heard before. At the same time I heard the music I also was being talked to and told all the answers to the universe (later I couldn't even remember the questions). An overwhelming sense of love generated out and within the bright light. I was told love was the basis of everything. I seemed to be traveling fast, yet in a slow way. Nothing just whisked past me. I saw and understood everything. Even though it looked like I was going through outer space, I was not cold or uncomfortable. I was not aware of feeling physically different than any other time. Even though I kept traveling up the tunnel, I never got up close to the light. I don't remember how I got back into my body, just waking up and instead of asking the nurse whether I had a boy or a girl, I said I knew all the answers to the universe. However, I learned quickly not to tell anyone what I experienced. For many years I put it out of my mind until while watching a TV show about near-death experiences, much to my husband and my amazement, we heard others talking about similar experiences."

Some of the most profound Near-Death Experiences are reported by children. Young children are innocent, open, and unbiased, and they seldom lie about such experiences. Many of them report seeing and hearing angels or deceased relatives who call them by name, telling them it is not their time to die. (12) Hearing these experiences has given many individuals hope and increased their faith in what they might experience when they die.

Our Near-Death Experience:
A few months after Cam's death, I felt impressed to call a friend and neighbor the night before his open heart surgery. I

told him that I knew his surgery was very serious and that his life was at risk. I requested that if he had a Near-Death Experience, and found himself in the spirit world, would he look for Cameron and give him my love? It was embarrassing to make such a request. He was very kind and said he would try to fulfill my request if such an event occurred.

However, he returned home from the hospital in good health reporting that he did not have a Near-Death Experience. Then an unusual thing happened. He had been home several days when he developed complications and had to go back to the hospital for an emergency gallbladder removal. He was very weakened by the first surgery and had to receive blood before he could have this second surgery. The medical staff feared he would not last long enough to even receive the needed blood. Fortunately he did. He recalls being awake during the surgery and hearing the doctors and nurses concern as they hurried about to resuscitate his heart.

He then felt himself being led to a large room, full of many deceased persons. He saw Cameron among them. He was walking and talking with another young man who appeared to be his missionary companion. Cameron appeared happy and busy, and apparently had important work to do. He tried to go to him and deliver the message, yet was restrained and led back to earth where he woke up in the intensive care unit. After the surgery, the doctors told him he had gone into congestive heart failure.

Although he was too ill to tell Dennis and I his story until many days later, he sent his wife immediately to briefly explain his experience. This was almost like a personal Near-Death Experience for us! It has been a comfort to have a glimpse of Cameron in his next life!

(ADE) AT-DEATH EXPERIENCES

At-Death Experiences have brought spiritual healing to those observing the event as well as those dying. Some dying nonbelievers say that they have seen angels or deceased relatives just prior to the death of a loved one. These experiences often convert them to the reality that there is life beyond death.

One interesting story involved a dying Chinese woman. She was talking about joining her husband who had died some years before. Then one day she was very puzzled. She asked one of the hospice nurses, "Why is my sister with my deceased husband?" The hospice worker talked with one of the other family members. She asked if the sister was dead. She was told that her sister was in China and had died just a couple of days before. The family had decided not to tell their mother for fear it would upset her. Following this event, they decided to tell her about her sister's death because they realized it would give her spiritual comfort and make sense in light of her vision as she faced death. (13)

Another dying woman awoke with a beautiful smile on her face as she reached for something unseen. She seemed to put her arms together as in a cradling position as she looked lovingly into her arms. As her family discussed this event, they realized that her first baby had died just moments after birth. She later had other children and the fact that she had lost a child was never discussed much. This was a very sweet moment for her family as they concluded that their mother was allowed to see and hold her baby as she died. (13)

When someone is dying, it is important that we pay attention to everything that they say and do because their communications may be subtle and symbolic. Some of these last communications could be missed because of our own preoccupations. Sometimes the important messages shared will be vague and confusing. Those present may think that the dying person is delirious or confused rather than trying to communicate something important. Common events occurring prior to death include dying individuals staring through you as if to see something else. In other instances they may seem distracted or offer inappropriate smiles or gestures, pointing or reaching for something unseen, and sometimes calling out names. They may report hearing voices. It is not usually helpful to argue or challenge what the dying are seeing or otherwise sensing.

I was working in the hospital the same day that my paternal grandmother was brought in with heart palpitations. I went to her room on my break to feed her dinner. She visited with me and ate a little. At the end of her visit she looked off into the corner of the room and called out my deceased grand-father's name. We then discussed how she had missed him for the last ten years and how she was looking forward to being with him again. She died a few hours later.

Some dying individuals talk about getting ready to go on a trip. A pilot may talk about getting ready to go on a flight. It might be helpful to go along with the symbolism and ask, "Do you know when it leaves; can I help you get ready?" If we try to relate to the dying's world, it can help them experience a more meaningful and peaceful death. If we have trouble under-standing, it is okay to say, "I think you are trying to tell me something important and I am trying very hard to understand, but I am just not getting it. Please keep trying to tell me." Recently I was visiting a hospice patient that we had served for several months. During the past month she rarely communi-cated with her family or our staff. This particular visit I asked how she was. She said, "Not well, I've had a terrible crash." I asked her if she thought she was dying. She nodded her head yes. I asked her if she was ready to go. Again she nodded yes. I asked her if she was afraid and she shook her head no. We shared some additional special symbolic communication. She died a couple of days later.

Many will describe seeing a beautiful place and it is okay to say, "I'm happy that you see such a beautiful place and that it makes you happy." Others may reluctantly share their fears. It is important to address any concerns, past regrets, strained relationships, unfinished business, repentance, etc. Encourage the dying by telling them you want to understand what they are saying. You might ask them, "Can you tell me more?" Pace yourself and don't push them. Let the dying control the conversation. One man described missing his trolley. A wise hospice nurse told him that she was sure that the trolley would stop for him soon and that he would be able to get on. The trolley was his symbolic way of saying, "It is time for me to go." It wasn't long after that he died. (13)

It has also been helpful to believe those who die are no longer suffering. They are in a beautiful after-world. It is those of us left behind that struggle through the loss and grief issues. President Kimball reminds us that the Lord does not view death as a curse or a tragedy. (14)

"Blessed are the dead that die in the Lord." (D&C 63:49)

At times because of the veil over our eyes and our limited understanding, it is sometimes hard to realize that:

"Those that die in me shall not taste of death, for it shall be sweet unto them." (D&C 42:46)

However, the Lord realizes the pain we experience in losing our loved ones. He makes us the following reassuring promise about the Millennium and our next life:

"There shall be no sorrow because there is no death." (D&C 101:29)

He also counsels us to:

"Weep for the loss of them that die...more especially for those that have not hope of a glorious resurrection." (D&C 42:45)

He has left us The Comforter and promises:

"....blessed are all they that mourn, for they shall be comforted." (3 Nephi 12:4; Matt. 5:4)

DEATH, CLICHES AND SPIRITUAL INJURY (also see p.16, 126, 234)

After the death of a loved one, family and church members often reach out in a sincere attempt to comfort those left behind. Unfortunately, sometimes their intended words of encouragement cause spiritual injury. The following statements and cliches resulted in spiritual injury according to these members who received them. We may believe these cliches and some of them may be doctrinally true. However, bereaved members list them as being very hurtful. Some of their specific responses are included in parentheses. These experiences and responses can help us understand and respect the vulnerability of the newly bereaved.

A friend said this to a mother the day her daughter died: "I just know one day you'll wake up and be all over this!" She replied with anger, "I will never get over the death of my daughter." A relative needed a favor and said the following to a mother whose only daughter had recently been killed in a car crash: "I had a hard time finding someone to help me who didn't have a lot of kids and then I thought of you." She still did the favor in spite of the thoughtless and painful reminder that her child was dead. A mother who lost a child wrote: "The man who drove the car and survived the crash in which my daughter was killed has several living children. His wife said, "Look for the silver lining behind your child's death and you'll find it because I did!" She went on to point out, "You still have your boys." (Those who have not experienced their own major loss often minimize the impact of such a loss in the lives of the bereaved!) Another bereaved parent was told by a temple matron, "Your son would be moving out and going on his mission in a few years anyway. This just makes it a little sooner." This mother said, "I felt like I had been slapped in the face." (Those of us who have had a child marry, sent out a missionary and also lost a child through death recognize that there is little comparison.)

This father lost an adult son leaving a wife and baby:

"About two months after the death of our son we had not heard from some really good friends. I stopped by and mentioned how much we were struggling, to which the husband said, 'Oh, I forgot.' I was so hurt and angry I left. We never heard from them again!"

"I was called to be the Stake Primary president. The next day my daughter away from home at BYU died suddenly. My father died eighteen days later. Three days after returning from all the traveling and funerals I had my first stake leadership training. However, no one in the Stake Presidency said a word to me about how difficult this all must be, having a new calling, presenting, etc. so soon after the death of my daughter and father.

"Fortunately I was able to make a good presentation. However, the pain from their lack of concern has remained with me. Four or five months later, while being interviewed by a member of the stake presidency, the subject of my daughter's death came up and I got emotional. The counselor said, 'Oh, you're not over that yet?' I bravely tried to explain that it wasn't something I would 'just get over,' rather I would learn to cope with it."

A bishop's wife posed this question to a father who had just lost a child:

"Isn't it odd how Heavenly Father takes the most precious?" This father disagreed as he reflected on the murderers, rapists, thieves, drug and alcohol addicts that die daily.

However, there may be circumstances when some appear to be called home. The Prophet Joseph Smith taught:

"The Lord takes many away, even in infancy, that they may escape the envy of men and the sorrows and evils of this present world..." (18 p. 196)

It may comfort some to know that their deceased loved ones are freed from the trials of earth life. However, others may become angry or confused. Some will ask, "Would God physically TAKE my child or does he allow these accidents and disease to occur even among the innocent?" A man was told by his elderly mother that a young girl in her ward was receiving messages from his deceased child. He declined hearing the messages, stating that he didn't want to receive messages from someone he had never met, and that he didn't think God or his daughter would work in that fashion. Another family writes what their Young Men's president said:

"Your daughter was chosen to die because of her special talents and God had a special work for her to do." The parents thought, but didn't say, let your own daughter do that special work and I'll send mine to the spirit world later!

A Young Women's leader spoke at the funeral and made this statement:

"Her death was not an accident or mistake, God is in

control, and if she didn't die this way, it would have happened another way. Her mission was finished." Her mother thought, I wished she hadn't taught false doctrine at my daughter's funeral. President Kimball feels that accidents can occur causing lives to be shortened. (14)

"A month after the death of our adult son, a brother training to be a counselor said to us, 'You really ought to be moving on now.' We thought, 'He doesn't understand and needs a lot more training!'"

"About six months after the loss of my daughter a good friend at church said, 'Are you still upset over that?' I tried calmly to explain I would always be upset that my daughter is gone."

A young men's president said:
"Heavenly Father needed your son, and he was well-prepared to answer the call." His father thought, "Send your own worthy son. I want to finish raising mine here."

A well-meaning Bishop said:
"It's surely a blessing to know she will be spared the trials of this life." Her mother thought to herself, "Send your child, it may seem like a blessing to you, not to me. I want to raise my daughter here on earth like the rest of you!"

The following statements were also made by members to the bereaved parents who shared them with us:
"Why do you go to the graveyard when you know he's not there?" "He's in a better place." (His dad thought, "What's the hurry? He was only fifteen.")

"You are such a strong person, how do you do it? I don't think I could handle it as well as you." (She thought, "You have no idea of the pain I'm experiencing inside.")

"You look like you're doing so well." (She shared later, "You can't see this kind of pain.")

"Your son is fulfilling a much higher mission now than was possible on earth."

"Well it's not like you don't know where she is!" (Her mother thought, "I would rather be worrying late at night for her to come home by curfew!")

"Well at least he isn't suffering, in a coma, or a vegetable. God loved him enough to take him." His father thought, "Does that mean God doesn't love my aunt who has been in a coma for over a year?"

(The "at leasts" usually don't help. They have the tendency of negating another's loss and grief.)

"God loved him enough to take him." (The sibling wondered, if I'm too righteous will he "take" me?)

"It was God's will," (see p. 139) "God needed him," "His work was done," and "It was his time."

All of the above "well-intended" comments are possible explanations for untimely death. Regrettably, even though we may believe one or all of these statements, they usually offer little comfort for those who are grieving.

The Holy Ghost can, of course, offer comfort through us when we are prompted: "Then can ye speak with the tongue of angels." (2 Nephi: 31:13) "Wherefore, they speak the words of

Christ." (2 Nephi 32:3) A Christian leader warned after years of observing the dilemma of sincere attempts to comfort that instead wounded those in mourning:

"We often bury more people outside the church doors than in the ground, when a death occurs!"

In other words, the bereaved are fragile, and at times things are said that hurt them, and in some instances drive them away from our church doors. It is safest in most instances to simply say you're sorry, and not "enlarge the wounds of those who are already wounded" with words of intended comfort that minimize the profound grief experienced by those coping with significant loss. (Jacob 2: 8-9) (For a list of helpful things to say see Ch. 13.)

A TIME TO DIE

"To everything there is a season, and a time to every purpose under the heaven: a time to be born and a time to die; a time to plant, and a time to pluck up that which is planted." (Ecc. 3:1-2)

Typical questions asked by those who lose a loved one are: Does everyone have a specific time assigned to leave earth life? What does "appointed time" mean? Is it a specific day, month, or year? What about those who die of sudden accidents? What about those who die as the result of murder?

Elder Kimball taught that we can die prematurely:

"I am confident that there is a time to die. I am not a fatalist. I believe that many people die before 'their time' because they are careless, abuse their bodies, take unnecessary chances, or expose themselves to hazard, accident and sickness." (14)

"Be not overmuch wicked, neither be thou foolish: why shouldn't thou die before thy time?" (Ecc. 7:17)

The Lord has told us that the sick will be healed if there is sufficient faith and "if the person is not appointed unto death." (D&C 42:48) Acts 17:26 says there is a determined time and appointed habitation. Hebrews 9:27, Job 14:14 and Alma 42:6 talk about being appointed to death. It was a comfort to some at Richard L. Evans funeral when President Joseph Fielding Smith said, "No righteous man is ever taken before his time." (4 Dec. '71)

Many dying have reported that during their near-death accounts they were told it was "not their time" and they had to return to earth. Some were even given a choice to stay or return. Recently a hospice patient of mine shared a near-death experience that he had a few years previously. After a surgical procedure he found himself out of his body, viewing it from above. Soon he was joined by a personage in white who reminded him of Moses. He was told that he must go back into his body because it was not his time to die.

Many dying patients seem to hang on waiting for a specific time to die. It may be a child's graduation, someone's wedding, the coming season, or a special holiday. It sometimes involves the completion of some important endeavor they have worked for. One Easter weekend three of our hospice patients died on Good Friday, three more on Saturday and three more on Easter Sunday. I've seen others who seemed to wait until someone who is traveling to see them arrives. It's important for them to say their goodbyes and have closure. Some seemed to hold on to life, hoping to make peace with someone that they had experienced relationship problems with in the past.

One woman seemed to hold on to life because her

husband was angry that she was dying. He was angry with God. After a talk with her husband, arranged by the hospice nurses, he realized he had to let go of his anger and give her permission to die. She peacefully passed away soon after their conversation. (13)

The Lord may also intervene and extend life. See Helaman 15:4,10-11 where the Lord "prolonged their days." Alma 9:16 indicates that the "Lord will...prolong their existence in the land." and D&C 5:33 promises "...that thy days may be prolonged...."

President Kimball said:

"I am grateful that even through the priesthood I cannot heal all the sick, I might heal people who should die. I might relieve people of suffering who should suffer. I fear I would frustrate the purpose of God." (14)

He also asked, "What if we did have power to heal? Would we have allowed Abinadi to die in the flames of fire?" Abinadi said:

"Touch me not, for God shall smite you...for I have not delivered the message which the Lord sent me to deliver...therefore God will not suffer that I shall be destroyed at this time...Ye see that ye have not power to slay me." (Mosiah 13:3,7)

After Abinadi delivered his message and was martyred he prayed, "Oh, God, receive my soul." As he cried, his face shone with exceeding luster, even as Moses did while in the Mount of Sinai while speaking unto the Lord. (Mosiah 17:19)

Enoch provides another example of someone being miraculously protected from death, "And it came to pass when they heard him, no man laid hands on him; for fear came on all them that heard him, for he walked with God." (Moses 6:39)

Lehi and Nephi, the Sons of Helaman, who converted

thousands, were also protected. They were put into prison without food. Their persecutors tried to slay them, but could not. They were encircled about as if by fire and they said, "...ye cannot lay your hands on us to slay us." (Helaman 5:26, 29)

Christ sensed when it was his time to die, "Mine hour is not come." (John 2:4; 7:30) As his martyrdom drew closer, he announced to His disciples: "The hour is come" (John 12:23) and "It is finished." (John 19:30)

An inspired bereaved mother, K. Larman, sums it up well, "Our destinies are determined day by day, based on the choices we make, we must constantly be preparing ourselves to meet the Lord whenever the day... whatever the cause of death." (K. Larman)

Elder Maxwell wrote:
"Although God is never surprised by unexpected arrivals in the spirit world, we must always distinguish between God's being able to foresee and His causing or desiring something to happen." (15 p.18)

THE FINAL HEALING GOD'S ATONEMENT AND RESURRECTION

"Life is real! Life is earnest! And the grave is not its goal; Dust thou art, to dust returnest, was not spoken of the soul." (Henry W. Longfellow)

Hope of a reunion with Cameron has helped Dennis and I endure. However, we still had to walk through a difficult grieving process. Soon after Cameron died I wrote the following. I can still hear the confusion and pain I felt that first year:

I knew I had faith, believed in God, and in life after death, yet in the beginning, I was shocked to find my faith was not enough to comfort me. I felt my son's soul still existed, yet when I saw his lifeless body on that cold hospital gurney, I wanted to know, not just hope, that he was well and happy somewhere. I questioned intensely, as did Job, "If a man die, shall he live again?" (Job 14:14)

I started intense reading, meditating and praying. I wanted to rediscover how I had gained a testimony of the resurrection. I studied Job. He struggled to understand, yet he bears a strong testimony of the resurrection:

"For I know that my Redeemer liveth, and that He shall stand at the latter day upon the earth: And though after my skin worms destroy this body, yet in my flesh shall I see God: Whom I shall see for myself, and mine eyes shall behold, and not another; though my reins be consumed within me." (Job 19:25-27)

Christ said, "In the world ye have tribulation..." (John 16:33) But He also said in the same verse "...but be of good cheer; I have overcome the world." He told his disciples, "...I go to prepare a place for you." (John 14:2) Our hope and belief in an afterlife does not rid us of our challenges and struggles; however, it can offer us great peace and solace as we endure them. "I am with you always to the end of the age." (Matt. 28:20)

Outside the LDS church we often hear the following questions, "Where is my loved one?" "When will I see them again? Are they safe?" Enoch asked similar questions when he "...beheld all the families of the earth; and he cried unto the Lord, saying: When shall the day of the Lord come... that all they that mourn may be sanctified and have eternal life?" (Moses 7:45) How blessed we are as members of The Church of Jesus Christ of Latter-day Saints to have been given knowledge of where we come from, why we are here, and where we are going!

"Why should it be thought a thing incredible with you, that God should raise the dead?"(Acts 26:8)

Joseph Smith said:

"If I have no expectation of seeing my family and friends again my heart would burst in a moment and I should go down to my grave. The expectation of seeing my friends in the morning of the first resurrection, cheers my soul and makes me bear up against the evils of life." (16 p. 85)

One night before Easter I was preparing a lesson I had to give on the subject of the resurrection to my Laurels at church. Cameron had been gone about one year. I had experienced a couple of dreams about him that year; however, they were usually about caring for him again as a young child. Easter morning I woke up early from a special dream, I felt it was different than a dream, more like a vision. Cameron was walking toward me. He had a beautiful smile on his face. He looked older (like he had looked in the casket) and my impression was that it was the resurrection. I didn't get close enough to talk or touch him, however, I felt the most peaceful and joyful feelings that I had experienced since his death. I look forward to the dream becoming a reality.

"For a trump shall sound both long and loud, ...and they shall come forth-yea, even the dead which died in me, to receive a crown of righteousness, and to be clothed upon, even as I am, to be with me, that we may be one." (D&C 29:13)

LOVING IN ABSENCE

We miss our son very much. We have had to love him in

"absence" because we can no longer love him in "presence." (17) Because someone has died does not mean the love or relationship ends.

We mourn for others who have lost loved ones. We look forward with great anticipation to claim the hope of the resurrection and see our son again: "Because I live, ye shall live also" (John 14:19), "...whosoever liveth and believeth in me shall never die." (John 11:26)

CHAPTER 11

MARITAL DISCORD AND HELP FOR YOUR MARRIAGE DURING ADVERSITY

"Marriage is demanding, but exalting. To miss the misery is to miss the joy. To miss the joy is to miss it all." (1 B. Hafen)

Many couples choose not to divorce in spite of marital discord. They experience grief and pain as they struggle to keep their marriage intact. Communication challenges and financial struggles are a major cause of divorce. Another common stressor among church members often resulting in marital discord occurs when one spouse is not as active or committed to the Gospel or their temple marriage as the other. Conflicts develop as they attempt to live with each other with their many spiritual differences and challenges. Differences that seem to threaten the eternal covenants are often the most painful to accept. It may start out as small differences, such as: how often do we pray together? How long do we fast? Should we read the scriptures together or separately? What kind of movies do we watch? How much time and church service do we give? What church events and activities do we attend? Any difference, spiritual or otherwise can bring conflict into a marriage. One spouse may feel hurt because he or she cannot convince the other to embrace theirs or the church's expectation of what is right or righteous. He or she may feel cheated or robbed out of a more ideal partnership as was imagined or expected before or during the marriage. This can lead to resentment and bitterness between couples. The other spouse may then feel judged, unloved, and condemned as not being good enough. It's difficult to "accept, not expect" in a marriage. Most marriages do better when couples tolerate each other's differences while recognizing, focusing and encouraging their spouses good qualities.

Some members feel they are suffering loss because of marital disagreements concerning living the commandments.

"I have thought of divorce off and on for years. The biggest reason is the lack of spirituality in our marriage. I finally thought our spiritual life was on its way because my husband of fifteen years decided he would give up his vices and take me and our children to the temple. I was thrilled. My excitement, however, didn't last long. A few months after our sealing, we bought a computer. My husband started spending time on the Internet. He has gotten into sexual conversations and pornography. I feel afraid. He has also stopped our scripture reading together and he doesn't read alone. He doesn't have much desire to attend church or the temple. I also feel trapped because getting a divorce would be more difficult now because we have a temple marriage. Does God expect me to love and accept this man when he is not living the gospel?"

"I know I should be grateful to have a spouse; however, I have always wanted to read the scriptures as a family. This has been a hard task to accomplish, as I am the only one who wants it to happen. The more I pushed, the more it seemed my family resisted. I finally realized that pushing so much was causing a great deal of contention in our home. With sadness and reluctance I let it go."

Expectations at how one's spouse will abide by the laws and commandments are often formed from childhood.

"I grew up in a family that seldom used cussing and profanity. However in my spouse's inactive family it was a common occurrence. After we were married I was surprised when words were used in anger that I had hardly heard before. I was hurt and offended. Both of us tried to adjust to what the other expected; however, habits from childhood are hard to break."

"I married a returned missionary who had been a convert. He served a great mission full of enthusiasm for the gospel. Upon return, he was zealous in his church service and living the gospel. I am not sure when I started fearing he would return to his pre-convert state or at least slacken in living the gospel commandments. I think it crept in slowly after many years of marriage. I feel scared because spiritual things have always been very important to me. It is hard to live with someone if you feel his spiritual goals are not matched to yours. I try not to be judgmental because I know I have faults too."

Many couples who marry belong to different religions.

"I joined the church after I was married. My husband has allowed me to practice most of my new LDS religion for twenty years now. I cannot pay tithing on his money, just on mine. He provided for our son to serve a mission and our daughter to be married in the temple. He doesn't want me to go to the temple because he doesn't want me to wear garments. He drinks; however, he doesn't pressure me to. He allows us to attend church on Sunday; however, afterward he expects us to do or go where he wants. It is very hard. I have thought of divorce off and on over the years, but have chosen to stay, hoping someday he'll convert."

Good marriages don't just happen. In fact, fifty percent of

marriages in the United States end in divorce. We were told in our 1999 AMCAP conference that temple-marriage statistics are several times better (although no source was given). (1, B. Hafen) However, the divorce rate for members is still occurring at an alarming rate. It takes hard work, compromise, tolerance and forgiveness to make a marriage work. There are Gospel principles, many that are listed in The Family Proclamation that provide support and direction to our marriages. There are also specific marriage practices that contribute to successful matrimony. (5)

When you add loss, stress, adversity and grief to your relationship, you can expect additional challenges in your marriage. One father said after losing a child:

"I not only miss my daughter. I miss how our lives used to be. My wife is not the same person she was before this tragedy and neither am I. We are suffering so many losses."

These bereaved parent's grief is so intense that their "physical or emotional symptoms and defenses block the growth in the relationship." (1 M.Gamblin)

Although now some professionals disagree, past research claimed that as many as eighty-five percent of the couples that experience the death of a child will eventually divorce. (2 p.84) Additional research has reported a seventy percent divorce rate for those couples parenting a child with a disability, or chronic/terminal illness. (3 p. 208) Whether couples divorce or not, the reality is there is an increase of stress within the marriage.

When a marriage fails as a result of the stress experienced from a loss it is called a secondary loss. The accumulative grief resulting from these multiple losses can be devastating to families. However, if we allow each family member to fully mourn and deal with their grief, they can usually love and live well again.

INCONGRUENCE IN THE WAYS MEN AND WOMEN HANDLE GRIEF

It is helpful to understand some of the basic needs of individuals in a marriage relationship: 1. Affection and Touch 2. Acceptance and Belonging 3. Communication 4. Friendship, Freedom and Fun 5. Security and Trust 6. Sexuality 7. Spirituality 8. Basic Physical Needs (food, shelter etc.)

When men and women are ask to prioritize these needs in order of importance, we often find striking differences. It is helpful for couples to understand how contrasting their preferences are. Grieving styles can also be unique. In addition to men and women's biological differences, young girls are often raised with different expectations than boys. For instance, boys are generally encouraged to be strong and silent, while girls are encouraged to express emotions. Society encourages numerous divergent roles for men and women that become blended with cultural and other stereotypes.

The following four P's elaborate on some of men's typical reactions to loss:

1. PROTECTORS: Men learn early that their primary role in society is to protect their family and property from harm. "When our daughter died, I felt as if I had failed to protect her. I think there were things I could have done to prevent what happened." Men also feel a specific responsibility as patriarchs in their homes. When adversity occurs, men often feel a sense of failure. A father may have prayed, fasted and offered blessings that haven't seemed to help. Watching his wife or family suffer due to a major loss constitutes a secondary loss for men.

2. PROVIDERS: Men often feel more responsible for the finances than women. It is often the man who returns immediately to work after a tragedy. The mother may stay at the

198

hospital or care for the other children at home. A man may push his grief aside to work the long hours he perceives are needed to support his family. He also may use his work to escape the painful realities of his adversity. One woman said: "I couldn't understand how he could just go right back to work after such a tragedy."

3. PROGRAM CONTROLLERS: Both men and women like control. However, men generally cannot handle feeling helpless or out of control. They may feel ultimately responsible for the house, yard, cars, and other temporal needs. With tragedy comes the fear of losing control over their stewardship. Their assumptive world has been assaulted. (4) "The sense of loss is, at times, almost overwhelming to me (loss of control)." Women frequently report feeling overwhelmed when confronted with the realization that there is not enough time to do all that is required.

4. PROBLEM SOLVERS: Men are often programmed more than women to "fix" everything. Some feel responsible for finding a cure or solution. When men or women learn they cannot fix or change their circumstances, they feel a sense of failure and guilt. Men seem to struggle when they feel power-less. One man writes after the drug-induced death of his son: "I was so mad at our son for putting us in this position. I felt guilt at not being able to help him with his problems."

It may be helpful for couples to realize that differences between men and women are common, and that it will take time, energy and healthy thought processes to work through all their unique grief issues during adversity. It may also be helpful to remember that:

"Husbands and wives each have needs for closeness and separateness. Problems erupt when one person's need for closeness threatens the other person's need for separateness." (1 M. Gamblin)

Remember that crying is only one of the ways individuals feel or show grief and sorrow. In our culture, men often grieve through work, activity, tasks and thoughts. This does not suggest that they are not grieving, and it does not necessarily mean they have unresolved grief issues. Grief can become apparent in many ways. A mother of a terminally ill child writes of these differences:

"Before we were diagnosed, we had a good relationship, and got along very well. During the diagnosis process we were both shocked, scared and ignorant about the facts. We started having a little tension between us. My husband and I have been raised differently. I have a lot of questions, but my husband accepts things and goes on. I had some resentment toward him because there were no tears, no screaming, no emotion! He just accepted it. I couldn't! Now that we both have finally accepted the diagnosis, things are okay, but still tense. I quit my job and became a full-time housewife and mother. My husband brings home the money. It is such a financial struggle, but we don't have much choice. We will all make it through this with God's help."

It is helpful to understand that men and women's bodies are biologically different. There also seems to be a difference in how men and women's brains function. These functional differences can affect thoughts, moods and behaviors. Men and women additionally have different hormones that influence feelings and behaviors.

One theory that addresses some of these differences suggests that more men than women are "left-brained dominant", functioning more with logic, factual and objective reasoning. Women are generally "right-brained dominant," relying more on their intuition to make decisions and cope.

They are generally more interested and concerned about happenings at home, relationships, and details. (I have to remind Dennis and the boys in our family that I need more details!) Generally women are more tender, emotional, nurturing, and talkative than men. John Gray, author of *Men are from Mars, Women are from Venus*, estimates that men speak about two thousand words per day while women speak about six thousand words. Men often use up their two thousand words at work, which explains their silence at home! Mothers and homemakers who spend their days with children may have most of their six thousand words left when her husband arrives home, tired from all his work-related adult conversation and ready for peace and quiet! If a man can listen and validate the women's feelings, and if a women can avoid pressuring her husband to speak or answer her immediately, their relationship will develop more smoothly.

Men and women evaluate their lives from different paradigms. Women generally see their lives as a "whole." If something goes wrong, a small flaw in her life, personality, or behavior, she often judges herself (her whole life) harshly. This is called "all or nothing thinking". An example might be a sister teaching a Relief Society lesson. She has worked on her lesson for weeks, has beautiful visual aids, handouts, etc. However, when the tape recorder fails her, she leaves feeling discouraged, thinking her whole lesson was ruined. If you go down the hall the same Sunday to the High Priests Quorum, you might find that a quorum instructor has forgotten all together that it was his turn to teach. He calmly asks if someone brought their manual which he borrows and the brethren begin to discuss the lesson. He and most of the other men go home thinking the class went well while debating and kidding about who will win the Super Bowl! Men often view, evaluate, and segregate their conflicting thoughts and behaviors individually into independent compartments of their consciousness. For example, a man can be a wonderful father and church leader and still not feel guilt from speeding on the highways or cussing and losing his temper during a church basketball game. The predisposition of not focusing on conflicting behaviors diminishes feelings of guilt. Men are usually able to view their overall life and self positively even when they struggle and fall short in certain areas. Women, on the other hand, seem to focus more on their weaknesses and are not as likely to rationalize or ignore their faults as easily as men. When you add all these differences to other variables such as family background, coping style, personality, past modeling, beliefs and values, you can see why a husband and wife may react or grieve differently over the same experience and loss. A mother raising a disabled child while fearing she's carrying a Down's Syndrome baby, writes to her deceased two-year-old daughter:

"I think I would be able to handle things a lot better if I knew this baby was O.K. Is it O.K.?...I keep thinking over and over of the night you died. It breaks my heart! Am I missing something, am I forgetting something, did I do something wrong to make you die, to leave us? Why did we lose you? You were the best thing to happen to our family. The other two kids have had a lot of problems lately. What is to become of us? Can we ever feel peace and joy in this life ever again? It is so hard for me to talk to people in the ward about my troubles. They don't understand, EVEN DADDY DOESN'T UNDERSTAND HOW I FEEL! I love you. Mom" (8 p.116)

Prophets have spoken on the different roles of men and women in a harmonious marriage. The Family Proclamation to The World (5) declares that children are entitled to be "reared by a father and a mother who honor marital vows with complete fidelity," and that "successful marriages and families are established and maintained on principles of faith, prayer, repentance, forgiveness, respect, love, compassion, work, and wholesome recreational activities". Members of our Texas stake were asked by our stake president to memorize The Proclamation. Studying these sacred words has had a powerful positive impact on our lives and the lives of many of the families in our stake.

What we like to refer to as the FOUR MARITAL C's can significantly influence and strengthen marriage relationships during stress:

1. Commitment 2. Communication 3. Cooperation and Tolerance 4. Conflict Resolution.

1. *Commitment*: Being committed to each other and the marriage is a powerful ingredient found in marriages that endure serious life challenges. Those who do not consider divorce as an option are more likely to find mutually acceptable solutions that help keep their marriages intact.

2. *Communication*: Historically, lack of communication has remained the number one cause of divorce. When couples are exhausted, stressed or mourning, it is difficult to find the time and energy vital for interaction. Remaining open, honest and frequently discussing trials and challenges will enhance meaningful communication.

It's important for men to remember that most women process their thoughts, concerns and decisions verbally. They think out loud, and say things they don't necessarily mean and espouse solutions when they are actually questioning. Women, on the other hand, need to understand that a man often processes thoughts and ideas silently. It may take him several minutes, an hour, or longer before he is able to reveal his inner-most feelings in verbal answers to his wife's questions.

During adversity we may find ourselves irritable and impatient. If we can focus our anger and disappointments on the challenges and issues rather than each other, we can stay connected. Allowing for the expression of negative and ambiva-lent feelings can be healing. When our repressed feelings are not expressed verbally and openly they become expressed in other ways. Unfortunately, these repressed feelings often resurface in the form of unhealthy mental, emotional or phys-ical challenges and illnesses.

The following simple technique can enhance communi-cation through the use of "I messages."

I feel_____ about_____ because_____ (6 p. 3.3)

" I FEEL sad and lonely ABOUT you spending so much time at work, BECAUSE I'm worried that you don't enjoy spending time with me."

A healthy response could utilize reflective listening to repeat back what was said to clarify understanding: "You FEEL I don't love you BECAUSE I seem more concerned with my work than you?"

3. *Cooperation and Tolerance*: It's hard for some of us to accept and share our feelings because we fear being labeled. Acknowledging and validating feelings and opinions is more valuable than attempting to judge those feelings and opinions as being right or wrong. Our feelings are usually present for a reason. Negative feelings often go away more quickly when *ACCEPTED* and *EXPRESSED*. We can avoid discounting each other's true feelings by avoiding the use of communication

roadblocks such as "Yes, but...", *shoulds* or *shouldn'ts,* etc.

Cooperation and "giving in" can break down barriers and power struggles.

Many professional therapists have discovered that "Tolerance Therapy" saves more marriages than other conventional therapies. Usually we cannot change our spouses; however, we can focus on accepting them and changing ourselves.

4. *Conflict Resolution*: "Sometimes our inabilities to resolve conflict keeps love out of a marriage". (7 10/ 96, p. 51) All marriages have conflicts, and not all issues can be solved easily. It is helpful to know and understand each other's family backgrounds, past losses and personal struggles. We bring many personal issues to our marriage. Any difference can cause a conflict, especially where our values, beliefs and spirituality are concerned. Couples may have to *AGREE* to *DISAGREE* on some issues.

PATIENCE AND FORGIVENESS (see p.148)

The following quote adds additional evidence concerning the value of tolerance, patience and forgiveness:

"Because so many marital challenges involve a needed change of heart, repentance, and sometimes careful rebuilding of the relationship; partners who wait patiently through the process are a great strength and blessing to their spouses." (7 10/96 p. 51)

"Waiting patiently on the Lord,....all things wherewith you have been afflicted shall work together for your good." (D&C 98:2-3)

TOUCH

Touch can be a healing tool for many. Massage therapy has been a healing art for centuries. It can bring comfort to those who are grieving emotionally or those who are terminally ill.

Touch helps couples stay connected. Touch can dissolve anger, frustration, and melt away tension. Touch or massage therapy can, but does not have to, involve sexual intimacy in marriage. One partner may find comfort in intimacy during loss. Touch, tenderness, and intimacy serve as a reminder that all is not lost. Others, however, may not be able to participate in physical intimacy during or immediately after a crisis.

The following touch technique may help relieve grief and bridge the gap between partners. Couples will need to plan to be alone, undisturbed, for about an hour. Realize this time together is one of the most important exercises that can be done to sustain a relationship.

Each partner takes turns massaging the other. Start with the back and neck, then move onto limbs, hands and feet. Lotions or oils can be used if desired. Rub deep into grief-stricken muscles. Couples can talk about their concerns, or just take the time to totally relax in silence. After spending this time together most individuals will function better emotionally and cognitively. Some couples will also notice over time a decreasing or softening of their grief, anxiety and stress.

It's important for couples to get away and spend quality time alone together. A weekly date, over time, is worth the money and effort. Many years ago our stake president counseled the members of our California stake to only borrow money for two things, "a home and a DATE"! He also encouraged couples to spend a night away together when possible. His counsel has had a profound and positive impact on our marriage. Communication and conflict resolution cannot occur if effort is not made to be alone together on a regular basis.

CHAPTER 12

HELPING PARENTS AND CHILDREN THROUGH GRIEF AND ADVERSITY

A crisis has impact on the identity of the family as a whole as well as each individual. Adversity has been known to pull a family together or apart. Parents and children often respond differently to the same experiences and loss.

Most children report that it is hard to talk to their parents during and after a tragic event. Parents are often unable to respond to all their children's needs because of their own grief issues. Children often must mourn the loss of their parent's attention, as well as the other unpleasant losses associated with the tragedy (secondary losses). Another example of significant secondary losses occurs when a child's parents divorce. The child may have to relocate, leaving behind home, school, friends, etc. Secondary losses can become more difficult to cope with over time, than was the primary loss. Often death, divorce, and illness result in the secondary loss of our traditional extended family. This loss of traditional families has been displayed over the years in several TV series: *The Brady Bunch* had two parents who were widowed. The father in *My Three Sons* was a widower. The father in *Bonanza* was a widower, and the *Beverly Hillbillies* starred both a widow and a widower.

Adversity can be confusing for children who may become angry at God or the church because they feel God should have prevented their tragedy or answered their prayers for healing. Spiritual injury is common and damaging when a child's prayer isn't answered how they think it should be, as previously evidenced by the young child who earnestly prayed for her parents not to divorce, only to watch them eventually divorce.

Parents should encourage (not pressure) children to express their feelings and fears by allowing them to be active participants in coping with the crisis, illness or death. Children can sense increased stress and anxiety in the home. They may feel and recognize that something is not right with Mom and Dad. If children are not told honestly or allowed to share in what is happening, they may become confused, frightened and insecure. Children feel secure when parents share feelings during regular family home evenings. They also feel comfort when parents talk, read scriptures and pray together. Including children in challenges doesn't mean parents should overwhelm them with their own grief, guilt, and unrealistic expectations. Children cannot fully comprehend a parent's pain. They have developmental limitations based on their age and limited life experience. Children may experience a loss of trust toward their parents, and identity confusion within the family unit, if important issues affecting the family are kept from them. Children look to adults, especially their parents, as examples of how to respond to life events. Seeing and sharing our grief in healthy ways often validates their own confusion and emotions. It's a challenging and frightening responsibility to realize that "parents can complicate or facilitate the grief process for children." (1)

A five-year-old was confused with her mother's change of behavior and mood. She would see tears in her mother's eyes, and ask, "Why are you sad, Mommy?" Her mother would reply that she was just tired because she was pregnant. What she didn't share was that she had found out she was carrying twins and knew one of the twins would not live due to a serious birth defect. This went on for a couple of months. A few days before delivery their doctor referred them to me. He hoped that some reading material and encouraging a more open communication style might help the family. After reading some grief literature, the mom told her daughter that two baby girls would be born, but that they could only bring home one sister because the other was sick and wouldn't live very long. This curious child asked many questions. When she got the answers she needed, she returned to her play. When the babies were born, she was allowed to see, hold and kiss them. The baby with the birth defect died a few hours later. As this five-year-old saw her parents and grandparents cry, she asked additional questions. When she had sufficient contact with both of her baby sisters, she turned her focus back to her crayons and dolls. The entire family spent time with the deceased baby sister. They had said a brief hello and now had to say goodbye. With time, everyone seemed to adjust to the loss, including the five-year-old.

"Children can't tolerate intense emotions for very long. Children generally have a short feeling phase." (2)

After his brother's death, our seven-year-old wondered: "Am I crying enough?" However, he was unable or unwilling to verbalize this guilt with us until he was fifteen years old. At sixteen he wrote a poem that was published nationally about an ornamental pear tree we planted eight-and-a-half years earlier in Cam's memory. We were surprised at the deep feelings and understanding that now at sixteen he could express:

The Pear Tree

Death, the disabled brother gone
Crippled, but much stronger than us all
Sadness and grief of the loss
Of a great brother, son, and example

Now planted in the earth his body lies
A small sapling also then planted
Small and weak, could barely stand
Weak as he once was
Year after year it grows
Stronger and taller it points to the sky
A remembrance of joys
That still live on
Beautiful, soft, white, flowers
Blooming on his day of birth
Falling to the earth
The month of his passing
The memorial Pear Tree
A true symbol of Cameron
Standing tall and firm above us
As he is now, while he watches below

Young children may ask questions such as: Does everyone have to die? Do you have to die? When will I die? Can we ever return? What do you do when you are dead? Why do people die? We should answer their questions as honestly as we possibly can.

Children are often robbed of consistency during illness, divorce and death. We shouldn't over-indulge them. We should give them our time and love. If left on their own without support and insight, they may blame themselves or feel responsible for the divorce, illness or death. In young children we may see bedwetting, returning to the bottle, clinging, and phobias.

Encouraging open communication may aid in the healing process. Remember young children communicate in many ways. Some may communicate subtly through behaviors and play. Others may communicate through art and music. Young boys often grieve through anger while girls become caregivers.

We can help children become healthy survivors rather than victims by offering support. We can guide children toward letting go of unrealistic blame and re-channeling their energies into meaningful and productive tasks. The following are age-appropriate characteristics of grieving children:

Children Two and Under: These children react behaviorally to stress around them. They can sense tension in the home and conflicts between their parents. They may react by crying, or through other changes in behavior such as eating, sleeping, bathroom habits, withdrawing, or temper tantrums. They respond best to consistent nurturing from significant others in their lives.

Children Three to Five: These children often react with similar behavior changes as those two and under. In addition, they may be very curious, asking lots of questions. Answer as simply and honestly as possible. We may see their grief as they color, draw, sing or play. Many children act out parts of the crisis with dolls and toys as they "play house." They may respond also like six-to nine-year-olds, feeling guilty that some-how they caused the crisis. We should allow them to talk and give them extra time and hugs.

Six-to Nine-Year-Olds: Generally they can understand adversity, divorce, illness and death. They recognize that death is final, they fantasize that divorce is not. They may feel their past bad thoughts, wishes, or anger toward an ill sibling or parent caused the illness or death. They need reassurance and reminders that others love them. They need hope for a positive future. They may experience negative dreams. We may see them acting out their loss issues through behavior problems or poor academic performance. Their physical symptoms can be similar to teens and adults.

Ten-to Twelve-Year-Olds: They may want more answers about what happened and why. They may kid or joke about divorce, illness or death to hide their true fears and anxieties.

Adolescents:

Teens can react as adults, with confusion, withdrawal, depression or intense emotions. However, because of their preoccupation with self they may not feel the depth of grief experienced by adults. Their recovery is often more rapid than adults.

"After my brother died I was afraid to talk to my parents. I decided to go back into the family room where my parents were. I remember sitting on the couch, listening to my parents cry. I didn't cry, I just sat there staring at the balloons that said, "Get well soon!" The next day and at the funeral it all got worse. I became more angry and depressed. I just wanted to speed up my life about two years and forget what was happening!"

We should avoid telling teens how they should feel or react. Lecturing, comparing, or over-controlling doesn't usually work. Although they understand death is final for others, they personally feel immortal. Consequently they may still participate in risk-taking activities as they search for their own personal identity. They understand that divorce is usually final. Adolescents are often self-focused, which takes most of their time and energy. They are also preoccupied with friends, and need our love and support to become free of peer pressure. They are concerned with day-to-day events, and may want to hurry time and get their lives back to normal. They need good role models, encouragement and a listening ear at crucial moments (often after midnight!).

Our eighteen-year-old son, who lives away from home, called to discuss his trials. I realized through this experience, how careful we need to be in responding to the misfortunes of children as well as adults. He told me that he had lost his girl-friend and his job all in the same week. As we discussed his sadness, I started asking him if he was paying his tithing, attending church, reading his scriptures, etc. He said, "Mom, I am not being punished". I thought about his statement off and on over the next several days. I wished I hadn't tried to shame or blame him for his adversity. Then one morning it hit me— my reply to him should have been, "No, you are not being punished, however, if you are keeping the commandments, you are entitled to the comfort and promptings of the Holy Ghost. God usually will not remove our trials, however, he can comfort us and oftentimes carries us through our most trying circum-stances and challenges."

Adolescents are often embarrassed by a parent's or sibling's illness, disability or appearance. (3)

"One day I had to make a quick run to my child's school. I just threw on a baseball hat to cover my bald head. When my child got home from school, he asked if I would please wear my wig when I came to the school."

These reactions and comments may later cause guilt, especially if death results. Discussing ambivalent feelings and helping families realize their mixed and—at times—conflicting emotions, may help them eventually abandon their guilt.

Some children, especially teens, may not want to be involved with the crisis, illness, or grief process. After Cameron died our teenager stated that he just wanted everything over with. He also commented later how it felt like we were a more normal family. He felt less embarrassment now as we traveled in public without the wheelchair, lift-equipped van, and without parents spoon-feeding his brother in restaurants.

Children may not be developmentally ready to process some aspects of the traumatic event. They may need to relive the experience or grieve at a later time as they mature and grow older. Our twelve-year-old son did more of his grief work years later in the mission field when he had the opportunity to work with a young girl dying from a brain tumor.

"Children's emotional symptoms may be slower in surfacing than adults, or even recur later when they reach young adulthood." (4 p.118)

We cannot force a child to grieve or react how we would like. We can be available to accept and guide them through whatever phase they are currently in, assisting them when and how they may need us.

"...available evidence suggests that not to assist the bereaved child in actively dealing with the death is to predispose him to significant pathology and lifelong problems." (17, p. 155)

Children, like adults, fear more bad things may happen. These fears can make them feel vulnerable, fearful and anxious. Seeing an ill sibling, friend, or relative suffer or receive medical treatments may arouse fears that they might catch the illness or need similar treatments. (19) They may ask, "What will my future be like?" "Who else will divorce, leave or abuse me, get sick or die?"

With time, reassurance, and love, a child's security can return. We can encourage children to talk and share only IF they want to. We shouldn't push them into feeling emotions or grief they don't have. We can help them memorialize the ill or dying by letting them keep something special that reminds them of their loved one. They might even want to perform a daily task or ritual. They could play a special game or listen to a favorite song together. Some children will enjoy rubbing lotion or oil on their ill loved one's feet or back. Participating in the event is a way of expressing love and concern. Others could help plant a tree, or buy a symbolic gift. These activities help children form special relationships with their loved one. The memories of these events can later bring comfort, special memories and reduce guilt. We can also allow siblings to be children, recognizing their need to play, laugh and fight during adversity. It is not wise to say, "Put it behind you, get over it," or "Be strong, don't cry." These statements encourage children to bury their feelings and promotes isolated disenfranchised grieving.

PETS

Caring for animals can be a healing tool for children and adults facing adversity. A pet offers unconditional love and acceptance which can be a source of great comfort.

Caring for animals also can help children learn that death is part of life. Losing a pet may be a child's first experience with loss. I remember how sad I was as a child when my pets would die.

After Cameron died Dennis and I got our children a dog. He has been an important part of our family for many years now. We will all cry and mourn when he dies. Adults as well as children bond tightly with their pets. Remember the song Bojangles? Bo and his dog traveled and performed together for many years. A strong bond was formed between man and dog as they worked side-by-side. When his dog died Bo became lost, depressed, unemployed and eventually turned to alcohol. (See words to song p. 239)

We shouldn't feel the need to immediately replace our

child's lost pet. We can provide them with the time and opportunity to cry and mourn. We can help them bury their pet. We can allow them to decide if and when they desire another pet. We should avoid the temptation to run and buy another pet in an attempt to negate the loss and stop our children from grieving.

CHILDREN AND FUNERALS

Children are exposed to eight thousand murders and more than one hundred thousand other acts of violence on TV by the time they leave elementary school. (5) They are rarely shown the aftermath of grief that inevitably comes following a death. Few are prepared to deal with the realities and consequences of a significant personal loss.

A funeral may help children actualize the event and their loss. Most children can attend a funeral. If they are old enough to love, they are generally old enough to grieve and participate. It is appropriate to ask them if they'd like to go. Explain what will take place, and what they will see. They could also participate in the program if they so desire. For example, they could write letters or songs to the deceased that could be shared if appropriate. Dennis and I left our four-year-old home during his grandfather's funeral. When he was fifteen-years-old he told us he wished we had let him go. We took our almost three-year-old daughter to her brother's viewing and funeral. When she saw her brother in the casket she said, "That's not Cameron." She was visibly upset and pushed to get away! We asked a friend to sit with her in the back of the chapel during the funeral, because she wouldn't sit still. Later, she didn't want to look at the pictures of her deceased brother in the coffin, the very same pictures that brought Dennis and I comfort. Fortunately, years later she remembers none of the negative events and seems focused on her pleasant memories of Cameron.

Some individuals, including children, grieve but do not mourn (it is helpful to do both). Mourning is often defined as the outward expression of loss, grieving is the feeling of loss and pain felt inside. Grief is the internal response. Mourning is what the public sees, the outward expression. Both grieving and mourning require the support and encouragement of others.

The function of funerals or other death rituals is:

To acknowledge the event and accept reality.
To remember and recall.
To receive support.
To express love and encourage emotional release.

TEACHING CHILDREN ABOUT AN AFTERLIFE

Studies show most bereaved parents of all religions believe in life after death. They hope for a reunion with their child. (6 p.35 & 18 p.65) The following analogy may help parents convey their beliefs and hopes in an afterlife to young children:

"Have you ever seen a butterfly? Did you know it was a caterpillar first? (Explain the cocoon and it's process.) Your brother's body lying so still (use words like *dead, dying,* or *die,* not *asleep*) is a shell left behind, like the cocoon when the butterfly leaves. His spirit or soul has gone or flown to another place, (heaven) just like the butterfly flies away."

Another visual aid helpful for young children requires your hand and a glove:

"This glove represents or is like your brother's body lying here so still in the casket." (Take your hand out of the glove and lay it down.) "The glove, like your brother's body is now empty." (Move your hand toward the sky). "Your brother's spirit, represented or like my hand, has gone on to another place we call heaven."

REBELLIOUSNESS

A child's rebelliousness may be his way of acting out his or her stress and grief. Raising rebellious or wayward children may also become a major loss for parents.

Often in spite of our efforts to provide a loving gospel-centered family, our children choose not to follow our teachings and examples.

"Why did I think I would escape having rebellious children? Why did I assume I was beyond enduring the heartache I had seen in other parents? Surely, I thought I was a better parent than they. How wrong I was to assume these parents had control and could have taught their children better. I had taught my child everything I knew to help her make right choices. I read her stories as a child, nursed her at my breast, cradled her curly head in my arms so tenderly, rocked her to sleep every night, and made sure that every playmate was suitable. I taught her to pray and to say 'thank you.' I avoided day care, I saw she lived in a good neighborhood. I fed her nutritious meals. I sang her Primary songs. We had weekly Family Home Evening. I sent her to good schools where I worked with her teachers. I taught her to keep her room clean, be responsible and work hard. I taught her not to steal and return things when she borrows them. She doesn't. I taught her to pay her tithing, but she won't. I taught her to live the Word of Wisdom, but she won't. I taught her to keep a curfew; she doesn't. I thought I taught her to show respect and obey which she isn't doing."

"Do we allow her to skip homework, pierce his ear, not pay her tithing, skip Seminary class, church or school? Can he date this girl or "hang out" with those guys? How should we discipline curfew violations or too many school tardies? How should we respond to the teen who refuses to do chores, or those who use drugs, cigarettes, or alcohol?"

One third of the high school students in this country get drunk once a week. Most teen suicides stem from drugs and alcohol. One out of four high school students use marijuana. One in four third graders report they have been pressured to try marijuana. Most adolescents get their first drug free. The biggest teen killer in the U.S. is alcohol.

"My son stays out late. He is always missing his curfew. He is seventeen and we have tried everything to encourage him to keep his curfew without much luck. I don't sleep well worrying about him. He has also shared with us that he has been involved with smoking and had some experience with alcohol. He does not seem to have a testimony or spiritual feelings. He is not interested in church, going only because we pressure him. We have talked with him, taken away money, the use of the car, etc. without much improvement."

Another father wrote:
"I was able to convince my seventeen-year-old son not to get his ear pierced. I said, 'Wait until you are eighteen, (he was seventeen at the time). See if it is really what you want by thinking about it for a while. When he turned eighteen, I said, 'Wait and see if you decide to go on a mission first. You prob-

ably won't want a pierced ear out in the mission field. Hold off for awhile and see.' He waited and obeyed. However, after he got his mission call, without asking us or with little hesitation, he went and got a tattoo. Another son seemed so irresponsible, riding a friend's motorcycle without a helmet, getting caught in a blizzard late at night in the mountains, totaling our car in an accident, taking things that weren't his, complaints from teachers, etc. One day he walked in with an earring. He hadn't even asked if he could get his ear pierced. He simply went and did it! He said, it was only five dollars and the lady didn't even care that we weren't eighteen!

Pierced ears and tattoos may seem insignificant to the parent facing more serious forms of disobedience. However, the pain and worry of being a parent to a troubled child can feel intense when the hopes, dreams and expectations for these children become shattered. It can feel similar to a death. (We can say this because we have lost two children to death and have survived raising difficult teens.) As we watch our children make choices that we feel are wrong we may feel life is out of control. It can be very draining. However, we must remember:

"No power influence can or ought to be maintained by virtue of the priesthood, only by persuasion, by long-suffering, by gentleness and meekness, and by love unfeigned; By kindness, and pure knowledge..." (D&C 121:41-42)

Some of us assume that once the diapers are gone and our children become teenagers, the load would lighten. However, raising teens can be like having a two-year-old again, only now the loss of sleep is from eleven p.m.to two a.m.rather than from two a.m. to five a.m. We can no longer make them go to sleep and they're too big to lift from their beds to wake them up. One of our sons wouldn't get up for early morning seminary regardless of how many times we went in and encouraged him. Then one day something changed. He started getting up with his alarm. We found out weeks later he was sleeping at the church on the stage! When asked by a teacher, "Why not just stay and sleep at home," he replied, "I get more sleep here at the church because my mom doesn't keep coming in trying to wake me up!

Another father struggling with one of his rebellious teens said:

"I am tired of fighting and trying to have a relationship with my son. He has so many behavior problems. Over the years his grades have suffered, teachers constantly call and complain, and we have caught him stealing repeatedly. I've tried to help him; however, nothing I've done seems to make a difference. He doesn't seem to care or respond to my counsel."

Boyd K. Packer wrote:

"The measure of our success as parents...will not rest solely on how our children turn out. That judgment would be just only if we could raise our families in a perfectly moral environment, and that now is not possible. It is common for responsible parents to lose one of their children, for a time, to influences over which they have no control." (7 5/92)

Elder Packer continued, quoting Elder Orson F. Whitney of the Quorum of Twelve Apostles:

"Though some of the sheep may wander, the eye of the Shepherd is upon them, and sooner or later they will feel the tentacles of divine providence reaching out after them and drawing them back to the fold...Hope on, trust on, till you see the salvation of God." (7 5/92)

It has been said that the greatest gift we can give to our

children is a loving marriage relationship. (See Ch. 11) If we are consistent, committed parents, we will have the greatest impact on our rebellious children. We must also agree on discipline and direction (Joint front). When one parent gives direction or discipline, the other backs and supports them with consistency and predictability. The exception to this rule would be the responsibility each parent has to protect our children from the abusive behavior of any caretakers, including a spouse.

Many parents have or will struggle and identify with Nephi of old when he said:

"For I pray continually for them by day, and my eyes water my pillow by night, because of them; and I cry unto my God in faith, and I know that he will hear my cry." (2 Nephi 33:3)

In brother Millett's book entitled, *Wandering Children*, he explains that if our children are sealed to us, we have claim upon the sealing covenant and promise that they will return to us, if not on this earth then in the next. (8) Remember, they were His "sheep" before they were our children.

I personally related to the following anonymous poem when I was a distraught parent with a rebellious child:

Where is My Wandering Boy Tonight?

Where is my wandering boy tonight? The boy of
My tenderest care; the boy that was once my joy
And light, the child of my love and prayer.
Once, he was pure as the morning dew,
As he knelt at his mother's knee; No face
Was so bright, no heart more true, and
None was as sweet as he.
Oh, could I see him now,

My boy, as fair as in olden time,
When cradle and smile made home a joy,
And life was a merry chime.
Go, for my wandering boy tonight, go search
For him where you will; but bring him to me
With all his blight, and tell him I love him still.
Oh, where is my boy tonight? Where is my boy tonight?
My heart o'er flows, for I love him, he knows,
Oh, where is my boy tonight?

I wrote in my journal the struggle I experienced with one of our sons:

"My rebellious son decided to move back home for a while. After about a week my patience has worn very thin. I am so tempted to ask him to leave home. It is so painful having him under the same roof, watching him make so many mistakes and throw so many opportunities away. One night when I was unable to sleep due to my worry for him, I turned to Jacob five in the Book of Mormon. I read about how long and hard the servant and master worked in the vineyard with the tame and wild olive trees: "What could I have done more..." (Jacob 5:49) (should I give up and burn the vineyard.) "But behold,....the servant said unto the Lord of the vineyard: Spare it a little longer." (Verse 50) The chapter spoke to my heart as revelation. I felt I had to be patient a little longer. This boy eventually repented and served an honorable mission."

It has also been helpful for me to realize that God lost a third of his children in the war in heaven. The scriptures say that He too, cried, wept and mourned with disappointment as he showed Enoch the wickedness of his children. (Moses 7:28,

29, 37) Enoch also cried, refusing to be comforted as he witnessed the loss of God's children. (verse 44)

Elder Featherstone suggests that parents who have wayward sons or daughters ultimately suffer more than anyone else. The point he makes is that losing someone to sin can bring about an eternal or permanent loss (this would also apply to the spiritual loss of any loved one). In contrast, when we lose a righteous loved one to death, we have a promise of being reunited with them in the resurrection if we are worthy: "Parents of a wayward one have a void and heartache that will not go away until the straying one returns." (9 p. 9) The parents of wayward children are often innocent of wrong doing; however, they suffer deeply watching their child stray. Elder Featherstone said, "If Christ can carry the burden of our transgression, it would only be 'just' that the innocent (parents) have their pain and afflictions removed." (9 p. 10) "I have no greater joy than to hear that my children walk in truth." (3 John:4)

HUMOR AND OTHER INTERVENTIONS

Humor can be an emotional release similar to crying during the grief process. Being a parent is an important and difficult task even when there isn't a major crisis going on within the family. I had challenges when I had a "full nest" as well as an "empty nest" I remember being very overwhelmed with my responsibilities as a young mother. Dennis was a busy bishop and we had five young children at home; one was a nursing baby and Cameron with cerebral palsy was in a wheelchair. I remember telling Dennis how overwhelmed I felt one day; then I said hesitantly, "I'm not sure if I even like kids!" Dennis turned a stressful moment into laughter by using humor. He put his index finger to his mouth, and said, "Shhhh, nobody does!" We both laughed and realized the importance of humor even in times of crisis and stress.

Preschoolers laugh about four hundred times per day. By the time we become adults, we have reduced our laughter to about fifteen times a day. (10 Vol.3 #7 p.7)

Parenting, of course, does have a serious side. In addition to the crisis, we may also be dealing with family traditions and struggles passed on from former generations. Some of the mistakes we make will also be carried into the next generation. An abused child may manifest distrust that contributes to failure in his or her own marriage. Children of divorce often become divorced parents. Generation after generation goes without a stable, loving, committed and healthy family. However, we can do some things to stop the cycle.

It is important to provide children with a happy and stable family environment during their grief. It is helpful for us to have a basic idea of what a healthy family is. Healthy families thrive most when parents and children communicate, listen, support, accept, laugh, respect, trust, compliment, play, work, serve, problem solve, pray and worship together. We are blessed and accountable to the inspired counsel found in the family proclamation:

"Parents have a sacred duty to rear their children in love and righteousness, to provide for their physical and spiritual needs, to love and serve one another...to be reared by a father and a mother who honor marital vows with complete fidelity." (11)

Sometimes it is helpful to ask our children what they need from us during stressful times. A mom and researcher interviewed more than five hundred children to learn the kinds of things children consider LEAST helpful. Here is what they said: (12)

1. *Indiscriminate praise*: EVERYTHING I do they tell me is good! Good trying, good finding, good breathing!

2. *Babying*: Whenever I go anywhere, they tell me "be careful".

3. *Not listening:* My dad doesn't seem to hear what I say.

4. *Not explaining*: They say they are going to be consequences but I have no idea what consequences are.

5. *Not showing you care:* Telling me all the things I need to do when I get home, instead of asking 'did you have a good day?'

6. *Making idle threats.*

7. *Public reprimands.*

8. *Nagging*

9. *Blaming.*

10. *Controlling.* Afraid I'll mess up.

11. *Bribing.* If you want this, you must do that.

12. *Over-scheduling.* I can never just hang out.

13. *Misplaced.* Ask them to do something and they will say, "Not now, we are busy."

14. *Negativism.* Too much criticizing.

15. *Ordering.* If I ask my mom why, she will say, "because I said so."

COMMUNICATION

The following comments are generally road blocks to communication and relationship deflators. 1. Not now! 2. You never... 3. You always... 4. Why can't you be more like... 5. Here, let me do that. 6. These are the best years of your life. 7. Stop crying. It can't be that bad. 8. Stop being so... 9. Act your age. 10. You were always such a good boy/girl.

Research indicates that children are most responsive when we have made more deposits of honest praise into our child's emotional bank account than we have taken withdrawals through criticism. (13) Honest praise can support children through their grief.

SELF-ESTEEM

A child's self-esteem and self-worth affects his thoughts and behaviors during the grief process as well as through out his life span:

"Those with low self-esteem often perceive a discrepancy between whom they are and who they would like to be." (14 No. 2 Vol.9-3) "Unrealistic expectations can also harm self-esteem." (15 No. 4 Vol. 4-4)

Everyone deserves to be loved and adored. All of us want to hear how wonderful we are and how much we are valued, especially during the grief process. We can offer this love and acceptance to our families, friends, neighbors and ward family. We can help others, especially, children focus on the things that they can do rather than the things they can't. This will lift their self-esteem and confirm their self-worth. Remember, we must learn to accept, not expect. This does not mean that we don't have rules or discipline for ourselves and our families. Children with low self-esteem often come from families where there are harsh or over-permissive forms of discipline. Most children respond best to clear, firm, consistent and loving discipline. Accepting ourselves, a spouse or child unconditionally is not always easy. It may mean "letting go" of control. Independence is the foundation of self-esteem and may be damaged by attempts to over control individuals.

Many children carry negative labels about themselves. "I am ugly." "I am lazy." "I am dumb." "I can't learn." "No one likes me." These self-defeating statements limit our children's abilities to cope and can damage their self-images. We can help displace these thoughts with new positive labels. Of course parents cannot shield a child from all negative situations. Peers, teachers, and siblings also influence the development of these negative labels. However, "Honest and open communication is the key to preventing self-defeating behaviors from developing and being maintained in our lives... ." (16 p. 161)

"Self-defeating behaviors based on faulty perceptions are kept alive and hidden within the individual when either good communication or sufficient love are missing.... In those stressful moments, people tend to say or do damaging things to children and let the damaging impressions stand unchallenged and unchanged in the child's mind." (16 p. 162)

Honest and effective communication is difficult to implement if we are too busy or angry. It's during these vulnerable moments that thoughtless or damaging words are often spoken.

"These negative concepts need to be talked out so that the child does not hold them as negative possessions that hinder individuality and limit or cripple potential." (16 p. 162)

Cameron did not have the talents and qualities emphasized in TV commercials that promise sex appeal, popularity, success or beauty. We tried to help him feel he was still a great human being just the way he was. I remember when a little boy asked if he could play with his new Christmas truck and horse. Cameron said, "Yes! ," hoping the boy would play with him as well. The young boy, just wanting the toy, said, "No, I don't want to play with Cam because he is ugly!" Cam responded, "I am not ugly!" (He really was a handsome young man.) He handled the situation very well. It was I who left the room crying! I didn't want my child and the others to see my tears and know that my self-esteem wasn't as strong as his! He helped teach our family the true meaning of self-worth and the value of each human being.

Ways we can damage a teenager's self-esteem
1. Putting them down.
2. Breaking promises.
3. Not allowing them choices and independence.
4. Not giving them respect and privacy.
5. Denying their feelings and identity.
6. Not being consistent.

CHAPTER 13

HOW CAN WE HELP OTHERS
FACING ADVERSITY?

Many individuals asked Dennis and I, "How do we help our friends, relatives, or ward members who are struggling and dealing with adversity and grief?" The scriptures give us the best answer:

"Weep with those who weep." (Romans 12:15)

"I was sitting, torn by grief. Someone came and talked to me of God's dealings, of why it happened, of why my loved one had died, of hope beyond the grave. He talked constantly. He said things I knew were true.

"I was unmoved, except to wish he'd go away. He finally did.

"Another came and sat beside me. He didn't talk. He didn't ask me leading questions. He just sat beside me for an hour and more, listening when I said something, answered briefly, prayed simply, left.

"I was moved. I was comforted. I hated to see him go." (1 p. 3)

MEMBERS HELPING MEMBERS SPIRITUALLY

As members of the church we have made a covenant to "...bear one another's burdens, that they might be light...willing to mourn with those that mourn; yea, and comfort those that stand in NEED of comfort... ." (Mosiah 18:8-9)

A religious leader explains why we desperately need support and comfort from our church leaders and ward family:

"For reassurance...our need for reaffirmation that God still does care for us, that God is still with us and that God is still forgiving and loving and merciful. Our world has crumbled and the one constant we need to be reminded of is the constancy of God's love, as shown in Jesus Christ." (2)

A member in the midst of loss expresses a commitment to remain active and forgive those who lacked empathy or failed to express it helpfully:

"I realized there were few people who could understand the intensity or duration of my grief. I felt hurt, angry, sad, and guilty on different occasions. I did not want to allow any of these emotions to drive me from my friends, family, God, faith, or church. With time, work, and patience, I, like many, found I could return with love and forgiveness to my friends, relatives, and family, who were unable to understand my grief. I was then able to offer help and support to others."

Some feel injured because of what they perceived God allowed or even caused to happen. To help them we must first accept and validate their feelings. When people tell us that they are not sure they believe the principles of the Gospel because of the hurt and pain they are experiencing, we must listen and assure them that this is a common part of the grieving process. If we try to rescue or reconvert them prematurely, it may only cause further spiritual injury. We need to overcome our fears that they are apostatizing and allow them time to rediscover or redefine their faith. We should refrain from prematurely pitting our testimony with theirs, or from giving them advice when they are not ready to receive it. When someone feels love and acceptance, they then feel free to explore the spirit and rediscover their God, church, faith, and testimony.

After someone experiences a crisis we may feel nervous the first time we see them. However, we should never ignore them or act as if nothing has happened. We should acknowledge their loss as soon as possible. A call, card, flowers or another gesture will mean much to those suffering. A physician who lost one of his own children said that before his loss, when he would hear of a child's death, he would send a card; now he sends himself.

Another way we can help the bereaved is to provide their basic life chores; cleaning, laundry, yard work, child care and cooking food are almost always appreciated. Also, if a death has occurred, attending the funeral of their loved one shows love, care, and concern.

Often we don't know what to say. A simple statement, "I'm so sorry you are having to go through this," is usually enough. Most bereaved individuals just want you to listen, listen, listen, acknowledge and accept their pain. If they have lost a loved one, be available to talk about their loved one and reminisce. Whatever the adversity, you might ask if they would like to talk about it; however, don't pry or ask for specific details. A helpful question might be, "What aspect is most upsetting or hurts the greatest regarding your loss?" Don't worry about making them cry. Oftentimes, that is what they need to do. Having someone they feel comfortable crying with can provide a beneficial release of pent up emotions.

"To weep is to make less the depth of grief." (W. Shakespeare from Henry VI)

We must avoid telling the bereaved how they "should" feel and avoid sharing our own experiences unless invited by those mourning. We should avoid saying, "We know how you feel," even when we have personally experienced similar challenges. Remember we are all unique and may experience the same trials differently. We shouldn't contrast losses by telling about someone else in a worse situation. We shouldn't expect them to "get over" their loss. We can let them know we'll help them *THROUGH* their difficulties as long as they need us. We shouldn't expect the bereaved to "call us if they need anything." They will seldom call, they are too overwhelmed and have no energy to reach out for our help. We must reach out to them for a longer duration of time than we have traditionally thought. Accept and acknowledge their feelings. Don't try to negate or minimize their loss or experiences by offering cliches:

Secular cliches:
1: You are young, you will have more chances.
2: Put it behind you, get on with your life.
3: Time will heal everything. (Time alone does not heal, what one does with that time can heal (grief work).
4: Be strong, keep your chin up.
5: Get over it, move on.
6: There are worse things.
7: Don't cry.

Cliches are not usually helpful for those struggling. We often say them because we've heard them ourselves and don't know what else to say. (For more cliches see p. 16, 126, 182) Even though those grieving may believe some of these cliches are true, the personal application must come from those experiencing loss themselves...not by others repeating them. Let the bereaved find their own "Whys". If a death has occurred, don't be afraid to share memories of their loved one's life. Remember that most people do not hurt by choice, they are trying their best to cope. It will be a long, hard walk for most. It may be overwhelming and frightening for many initially to think of living with such pain.

"We mourn in black: why mourn we not in blood?" (W. Shakespeare from Henry VI)

NON-AIDING AND AIDING EXPRESSIONS:

Let your concern and caring show.Don't expect too much and impose 'shoulds' on those in mourning.
Be available to listen or run errands.Don't let your own sense of helplessness keep you away from those hurting.
Say that you are sorry about whatever happened.Don't avoid them because you are uncomfortable.
Allow those grieving to express their feelings. Don't say you know how they feel.
Allow them to talk about and express what happened. Don't tell them how they should feel and that they should be better now.
Give special attention to siblings. Don't change the subject when they want to talk about their tragedy.
Allow them to do as much as possible for themselves. Don't avoid mentioning a deceased person's name.
Respect their need for privacy.

Additional *don'ts* to be aware of:

Don't try to find something positive about their tragedy, they can do that for themselves. Don't point out their blessings, they can do that for themselves.
Don't suggest that they should be grateful for other loved

ones.

Don't moralize or offer theology unless invited to do so.

Don't say things that will intensify feelings of doubt and guilt already present. Don't use cliches.

Don't give advice about what they should feel, there are no right or wrong feelings, they are just feelings.

Don't share things that were intended to be kept in confidence.

Don't tell them other stories of tragedy and catastrophe when they are already feeling vulnerable.

Don't make light of things sacred or meaningful to them.

Don't continually question their decisions.

Don't label their feelings or behavior as abnormal, childish, neurotic, etc.

Do not encourage self-destructive behavior.

Do not be embarrassed by tears.

Most importantly, remember—we can send ourselves instead of a card.

PROFESSIONAL HELP

Knowing when someone needs more than personal insights and self help tools is not always easy. If someone has an abrasion, cut, or a broken arm, we physically see the wound and send them to the hospital to have it treated. We put them on antibiotics and pain medications. When someone has a broken heart and soul, we can't always see it visually; however, those suffering adversity will often tell you their emotional pain hurts more than broken bones or other physical pains they have experienced. Because emotional wounds are not always visible, individuals often fail to seek the help they need. Often their body and soul has been damaged, bruised and shattered by their loss. Professional therapy may help. There are techniques designed to address specific types of challenges. Medications have also been improved and can help a great deal. If in doubt, seek professional help and advice. LDS Family Services offers counseling and referrals to LDS professionals in your community.

When one's emotions, thoughts or behaviors become debilitating, distorted, or exaggerated, professional help should be seriously considered. This would include when sadness turns to clinical depression (see p. 69), anger turns to prolonged bitterness or rage, fear turns to anxiety or panic attacks, and guilt turns to shame. Also, watch for siblings trying to take on grown-up roles, and children or parents trying to replace the deceased by acting like them. Self-pity, fear of failure or rejection, and prolonged inability to function at home, school, or work are also potential warning signs. The absence of grief can be another warning sign. Everyone is vulnerable to substituting something else for their grief process. Substitutes may include staying away from home, under- or overdoing, and any type of obsession or addiction.

If a child is struggling, seek help from a licensed professional counselor who has experience treating children experiencing loss. If a marriage is having difficulties, seek a marriage therapist, familiar with loss issues.

COVENANT BLESSINGS

Members of the Church of Jesus Christ of Latter-day Saints make covenants at baptism. We renew these covenants each week as we partake of the sacrament. Three of the eight promises we make as we partake of the sacrament have to do with serving others who are experiencing loss and adversity:

1. "Willing to bear one another's burdens."

2. "Mourn with those that mourn."
3. "Comfort those that stand in need of comfort."
   (Mosiah 18: 8-9)

May God give us the strength, courage, and commitment to keep these covenants, so we too may say as Paul:

"I have fought a good fight, I have finished my course, I have kept the faith." (2 Timothy 4:7)

Mr. Bojangles
by
The Nitty Gritty Dirt Band

I knew a man, Bojangles and he danced for you
In worn out shoes
Silver hair, a ragged shirt and baggy pants
the old soft shoe
He jumped so high
He jumped so high
Then he'd lightly touch down
I met him in a cell in New Orleans, I was
Down and out
He looked to me to be the eyes of age
As he spoke right out
He talked of life
He talked of life
He laughed, clicked his heels and stepped
He said his name, Bojangles and he danced a lick
Across the cell
He grabbed his pants, a better stance
Oh, he jumped so high
Then he clicked his heels
He let go a laugh
He let go a laugh
Pushed back his clothes all around
Mr. Bojangles
Mr. Bojangles
Mr. Bojangles
Dance
He danced for those in minstrel shows and county fairs
Throughout the South

He spoke with tears of fifteen years how his dog and him
Traveled about
The dog up and died
He up and died
After twenty years he still grieves
He said I dance now at every chance in honky tonks
For drinks and tips
But most the time I spend behind these county bars
He said, "I drinks a bit."
He shook his head
And as he shook his head
I heard someone ask him please
Please
Mr. Bojangles
Mr. Bojangles
Mr. Bojangles
Dance

Figure #1

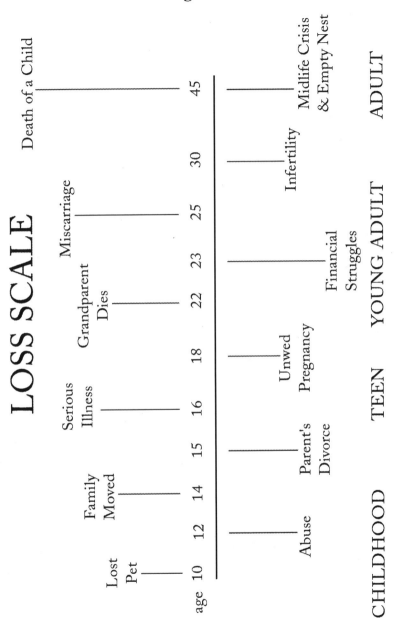

Figure # 2

COPING VARIABLES

Type of loss

Anticipatory time

Relationship to the loss

Personality

Sex, age and maturity

Coping abilities

Past losses and experiences

Physical, spiritual and mental health

Lifestyle and expectations

Intelligence and education

Beliefs and values

Family makeup, rules and expectations

Figure # 3

Five Dimensions of the Human System

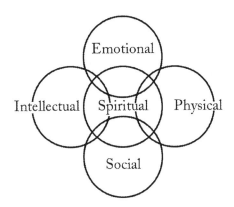

Grief Symptoms

PHYSICAL:

Changes in:
    appetite
    vision
    sleep
    weight
    bowels
    Sex
Muscle twitches
restlessness
breathlessness
heart palpitations
headaches
crying
exhaustion
dry mouth

EMOTIONAL:

Shock
Numbness
Anger
Fear
Confusion
Anxiety
Denial
Sadness
Disbelief
Yearning
Loneliness
Irritability
Depression
Relief
Guilt

SPIRITUAL:

Impressions
Dreams
Loss of Faith
Increase of faith
Angry at God
Spiritual Injury
Questioning values
Betrayal from God
Disappointment in leaders

SOCIAL:

Loss of Identity
Isolation
Withdrawal
Lack of interaction energy
Loss of ability to function

INTELLECTUAL:

Disorganization
Lack of concentration
Disorientation
Absent minded
Intellectualizing

References

Chapter 1

1. H. S. Kushner, *When Bad Things Happen to Good People*, Avon Books, N.Y. 1981.

2. R.K. Limbo and S.R. Wheeler, *When a Baby Dies: A Handbook for Healing and Helping*, La Crosse Lutheran Hospital/Gundersen Clinic, Ltd., 1986.

3.T.A. Rando, 1995. "Grieving and Mourning: Accommodating to loss. In Dying: Facing the facts", edited by H.Wass and R.A.Niemeyer, pp.211-43 WA. DC:Taylor & Francis.

4. Grollman, E. King's College Bereavement Conference, May, 1995.

5. Hospice Foundation of America's Newsletter, 'Journeys', Miami Beach, Fl. March 1999.

6. E.A. Grollman, *Living When a Loved One Has Died*, Beacon Press, Boston. Mass.1977, p. 58.

7. G.W. Davidson, *Understanding Mourning*, Augsburg Publishing House, Minneapolis, Minnesota, 1984.

8. Humphery, M.G. &Zimpfer G.D. (1996). *Counseling for grief and bereavement*, Thousand Oaks, Ca.: Saga Publication.

9. A. Bozarth-Campbell, *Life is Goodbye, Life is Hello*, CompCare Publications, Minn., Minnesota, 1982.

10. M.C. Sanders, (1999) *Grief the Mourning After*, N.Y. John Wily & Sons, Inc.

Chapter 2

1. B.D. Rosof, *The Worst Loss: How families heal from the death of a child*, H. Holt & Co; New York, 1994.
2. T.A. Rando, 1995. "Grieving and Mourning: Accommodating to loss. In Dying: Facing the facts," edited by H.Wass and R.A.Niemeyer, PP.211-43 WA. DC:Taylor & Francis.
3. Hospice Foundation of America, 'Living With Grief', National Teleconference, 4/14/99 speaker K. Doka.
4. J. Ashton & D. Ashton, *Loss and Grief Recovery*, Baywood Publishing Co., Inc. Amityville, New York, 1996.
5. B.R. McConkie, *Mormon Doctrine*, 2nd ed. SLC: Bookcraft, 1966, p.711.
6. G.Anderson, *Our Children Forever*, Berkley Books, New York, 1994 p.186.
7. Ballard, Russell M., *Suicide: Some Things We Know, and Some We do not*, Deseret Book Co. SLC 1993.
8. The Forum Newsletter, Association for Death Education and Counseling Mar/Apr 1999 p.15, J. Stanford.
9. Ashton's chapter 14, T.A. Rando, *Clinical Dimensions of Anticipatory Mourning: Theory and Practice in Working with the Dying, Their Loved Ones, and Their Caregivers*, Research Press, Champaign, IL., 2000.

Chapter 3

1.American Cancer Society, 1998 Cancer Facts & Figures 1998, Atlanta, GA:author
2. Ashton's chapter 14, T.A. Rando, *Clinical Dimensions of Anticipatory Mourning: Theory and Practice in Working with the Dying, Their Loved Ones, and Their Caregivers*, Research Press, Champaign, IL., 1999.

3. E. Kingsley, 'Welcome To Holland' broadcast by Television Works Western Publication Co. 508-750-8400.
4. J. Ashton& D. Ashton, *Loss and Grief Recovery*, Baywood Publishing Co., Inc. Amityville, New York, 1996.
5. The Forum Newsletter, Association for Death Education and Counseling May/June 1998.

Chapter 4

1. THE FAMILY: A Proclamation to the World, The Church of Jesus Christ of Latter-Day Saints, 1995.
2. Mayo Clinic Womens Healthsource, Boulder, Co. Vol. 3#3 and Vol. 3#7 1999.
3. V. J. Featherstone, *The Incomparable Christ*, Deseret Book, SLC, 1996.
4. Church News, Deseret News, SLC, UT.
5. CNN TV News 5/4/99.
6. G. B. Hinckley, Helping Others to Help Themselves, Welfare pamphlet, 1945.
7. Nurseweek Publishing Inc. 'Healthweek', Dallas/Fort Worth, TX, 4/12/99, p. 32.
8. CNN TV News 4/12/99.
9. J. Park, *Resolving Homosexual Problems,* Century Publishing. SLC, UT. 1997.

Chapter 5

1. D. Edwards, audio tape, Learning to Live With Grief, Covenant Recordings, Inc., S.L.C., UT. 1989.
2. DSM 111 Diagnostic and Statistical Manual of Mental Disorders (3rd Edition), American Psychiatric Association, Washington, D.C., 1987.
3. E. Kubler-Ross, *On Death and Dying*, Macmillian Publishing Co., Inc., New York, 1969.

4. B. Bush, Guilt-a tool for Christian Growth, Abbey Press, St. Meinrad, Indiana, 1991.

5. C. Thurman, *These Truths We Must Believe*, Thomas Nelson, Nashville, Tennessee, 1991.

6. G.W. Davidson, *Understanding Mourning*, Augsburg Publishing House, Minneapolis, Minnesota, 1984.

7. C. Tuttle, *The Path to Wholeness*, Covenant Communications, American Fork, UT. 1993.

8. ADEC, Association for Death Education and Counseling Conference, Chicago, Ill. March 1998 speaker A. Wolfelt.

9. R.K. Limbo and S.R. Wheeler, *When a Baby Dies: A Handbook for Healing and Helping*, La Crosse Lutheran Hospital/Gunderse Clinic, Ltd., 1986, p. 8.

10. B.D. Rosof, *The Worst Loss: How families heal from the death of a child*, H. Holt & Co; New York, 1994.

11. Sobel, D.S., 1997. "Partners in Health Newsletter". Kaiser Foundation, Dallas, TX.

12. M.Dickson, Grief Seminars, Dallas, Texas 1992

13. R. Neihbor (quote over 100 years old).

14. P.S. Buck, *The Child that Never Grew*, Woodbine House, Bethesda, Maryland, 1950, p.26.

15. J. Borysenko, *Minding the Body, Mending the Mind*, Addison-Wesley Publishing Co., Inc., Reading, Massachusetts, 1987.

16. K.J. Doka, *Children Mourning/Mourning Children*, Hospice Foundation of America, Wa. DC 1995.

17. AMCAP Association of Mormon Counselors and Pyschotherapists Conference, SLC, Ut. Oct. 1997.

Chapter 6

1. E.N. Jackson, *Understanding Grief*, Abingdon Press Nashville, Tennessee, 1946.

2. B.L.G. Morgan and R. Morgan, *Hormones (Brainfood)* The Body Press, Los Angeles, CA 1989.

3. Ornstein, R. Swenciconis, C. (1990). The Healing Brain. New York: Guilford

4. J. Borysenko, *Minding the Body, Mending the Mind*, Addison-Wesley Publishing Co., Inc., Reading, Massachusetts, 1987.

5. Wolfelt, A.D. (1996, August 22). *"Lessons in Caring for the Dying."* Workshop handout, Dallas Market Center.

Chapter 7

1. F. Nietzsche (quote public domain over 100 years old).

2. Frankl, V.E. (1946) *Man's Search for Meaning*. New York: Simon and Schuster.

3. "Big Rock Candy Mountains" Deseret News, 12 June 1973, p. A4 quoted in the Ensign, March 1997, "A Conversation with Single Adults" p. 58 Hinckley, G. SLC, Utah.

Chapter 8

1. Buscaglia, L., *The Disabled and Their Parents: A Counseling Challenge*. Charles B. Slack, Inc., Thorofare, New Jersey, 1975.

2. Radio talk show, Dr. Less Carter, Minirth-Meier Media Ministries, Richardson, Texas, 1994.

3. J. Borysenko, *Minding the Body, Mending the Mind*. Addison-Wesley Publishing Co., Inc., Reading, Massachusetts, 1987.

4. C. Tuttle, *The Path to Wholeness*, Covenant Communications, American Fork, UT. 1993.

5. Covey, S.R., *Principle-Centered Leadership*, Summit Books, New York, 1990-91.

6. AMCAP Associations of Mormon Counselors and

psychotherapists Conference, SLC, UT. April 1999, speaker M. Gamblin.

7. J. Chamberlain, *Eliminate Your SDB's* (Self-Defeating Behaviors), BYU Press, Provo, Utah, 1978, p.1.

8. J. Ashton& D. Ashton, *Loss and Grief Recovery,* Baywood Publishing Co., Inc. Amityville, New York, 1996. P. 52-3.

Chapter 9

1. Woodward, K. "Deadened for the Mainline." Newsweek Aug. 9, 1993: 46-48.

2. Ensign Magazine, 50 E. North Temple, SLC, UT 84150-3224, 4/99 p.78.

3. E. Grollman, King's College Bereavement Conference, May, 1995.

4. C. Meyers, *Surviving Death: A Practical Guide to Caring For The Dying and Bereaved,* Twenty-Third Publications. Mystic , CT 1991.

5. Burton, K.W. "When God is silent... Loss and Faith." Heartbreaking Choice Newsletter, Summer 1998.

6. J. Ashton & D. Ashton, *Loss and Grief Recovery,* Baywood Publishing Co., Inc. Amityville, New York, 1996.

7. ADEC, Association for Death Education and Counseling Conference, Chicago, Ill. March 1998 speaker A. Wolfelt.

8. Edwards, D. *GRIEVING: The Pain and the Promise,* Covenant, Inc., SLC, UT., 1989.

9. S.W. Kimble, *The Teachings of S.W. Kimble,* Bookcraft SLC, UT 1982.

10. *The Gospel Kingdom, writings and discourses of John Taylor,* Bookcraft, Inc., 1987 SLC, UT.

11. N. A. Maxwell, *All These Things Shall Give Thee Experience,* Deseret Book, 1979, SLC, UT.

12. Grollman, E.A., *Living When a Loved One Has died,*

Beacon Press, Boston, Mass. 1997.

13. S.W. Kimble, 'Tragedy or Destiny', Deseret Book, SLC, Utah 1982.

14. J. Hunt, 'Hope for the Heart' Newsletter Sept./Oct. 1996.

15. Old Testament Media video CES '91.

16. J. R. Zurheide *When Faith is Tested*, Augsburg Fortress, Minn., MN 1997.

17. H. S. Kushner, *When Bad Things Happen to Good People,* Avon Books, N.Y. 1981.

18. L. Cook, *Words of J. Smith* Deseret Book, SLC, Utah, 1984, p.15.

19. B.K. Packer, The Mediator, Ensign Magazine, May 1977 p.54-56.

20. Callister, Tad R., *Infinite Atonement*, Deseret Book, SLC 2000.

21. AMCAP Associations of Mormon Counselors and Psychotherapists Conference, SLC, UT. April 1999, speaker M. Gamblin.

22. Church News, Deseret News, SLC, UT.

23. The Compassionate Friends Newsletter, Carrollton-Farmers Branch Chapter Feb. 99, Dinah M. Mulock.

24. R.J.Hulbert, *The Sun is Always Shining,* Eptic Enterprises, Parma, Id.

25. AMCAP Association of Mormon Counselors and psychotherapists Conference, SLC, UT. Oct. 1997.

26. D. Tracy, *Plurality and Ambiguity: Her meneutics, religion, and Hope*, Chicago, IL.: Chicago Press 1987.

27. Kimball, S.W., *Faith Precedes The Miracle,* Deseret Book SLC, Utah 1972.

28. F. Nietzsche (quote public domain over 100 years old).

29. Kimball, S.W., *Faith Precedes The Miracle,* Deseret Book SLC, Utah 1972.

30. Bateman M. The Ensign magazine, SLC, UT. Jan. 1999, p.13.

Chapter 10

1.P.H. Dunn, *The Birth We Call Death*, Bookcraft Inc., Salt Lake City, UT 1976, p.12.

2. J. Ashton & D. Ashton, *Loss and Grief Recovery*, Baywood Publishing Co., Inc. Amityville, New York, 1996.

3. E. Linn, *Premonitions, Visitations and Dreams . . . of the Bereaved*, Publishers Mark, Incline Village, Nevada, 1991.

4. Ensign Magazine, 50 E. North Temple, SLC, UT 84150-3224.

5. J. Heinerman, *Spirit World Manifestations*, Joseph Lyon and Assoc. Dba Magazine Printing & Publishing, SLC, UT 1978.

6. Oprah Winfrey show produced by Harpo Productions, Inc., Chicago, Il., Oct. 8, 1993.

7. M.R. Sorenson and D.R. Willmore, *The Journey Beyond Life*, Vol 1, Sounds of Zion, Inc., Midvale, Utah 1988.

8. Trial by Terror, Wixom; LA Times, May 16-18, 1986; School Administrator Magazine, 48, pp. 12-17, May & June 1991; Also CBS Broadcast, 4/5/94 Save the Children.

9. Hyrum G. Smith, Conference Report, April 1917, p. 70-71.

10. L.E. LaGrand, *After Death Communications,* Llewellyn Publica, St. Paul, MN 1997.

11. Otten & Caldwell, Sacred Truths of the Doctrine & Covenants, Vol.1, p.63.

12. M. Morse, *Closer to the Light*, Villard Books, New York, 1990.

13. M. Callanan & P. Kelley, *Final Gifts* Bantom Books, 1992 NY, NY.

14. S.W. Kimble, 'Tragedy or Destiny', Deseret Book, SLC, Utah 1982.

15. N. A. Maxwell, *All These Things Shall Give Thee*

Experience, Deseret Book, 1979, SLC, UT.

16. Book of Mormon Student Manual, Religion 121 & 122, p. 85, Church of Jesus Christ of Latter-day Saints, SLC, Utah 1989&1996.

17. T.A. Rando, *Clinical Dimensions of Anticipatory Mourning: Theory and Practice in Working with the Dying, Their Loved Ones, and Their Caregivers*, Research Press, Champaign, IL., 2000. (Attig chapter 4).

18. *Teachings of the Prophet Joseph Smith*, Deseret Book, 1976, SLC, UT, p. 196.

Chapter 11

1. AMCAP, Associations of Mormon Counselors and Psychotherapists Conference, SLC, UT. April 1999.

2. N. Cycol, Pediatric Nursing Symposium, Children's Medical Center, Cook Country, Fort Worth, TX 1992.

3. F. Kupfer, *Before & After Zachariah*, Delacorte Press, New York, 1971.

4. Ashton's chapter 14, T.A. Rando, *Clinical Dimensions of Anticipatory Mourning: Theory and Practice in Working with the Dying, Their Loved Ones, and Their Caregivers*, Research Press, Champaign, IL., 1999.

5. THE FAMILY: A Proclamation to the World, The Church of Jesus Christ of Latter-Day Saints, 1995.

6. Becoming a Better Parent, L.D.S.S.S manual., SLC, UT. p. 3.3, 1976.

7. Ensign Magazine, 50 E. North Temple, SLC, UT 84150-3224.

8. J. Ashton & D. Ashton, *Loss and Grief Recovery*, Baywood Publishing Co., Inc. Amityville, New York, 1996.

Chapter 12

1. Hospice Foundation of America, 'Living With Grief', National Teleconference, 4/14/99. K. Doka, speaker.

2. ADEC, Association for Death Education and Counseling Conference, Chicago, Ill. March 1998 speaker A. Wolfelt.

3. Faux, S.A. Sibling Relationships in congenitally impaired children. *Journal of Pediatric Nursing*, 6(3), 175-184. 1991 Edition.

4. J. Ashton & D. Ashton, *Loss and Grief Recovery*, Baywood Publishing Co., Inc. Amityville, New York, 1996.

5. Children Television and Violence 1998.

6. Knapp, R.J. *Beyond Endurance-When a Child Dies*, New York: Schocken Books, (1986).

7. Ensign Magazine, 50 E. North Temple, SLC, UT 84150-3224.

8. R.L. Millett, *When a Child Wanders.*, Deseret Book, SLC, Utah 1996.

9. V. J. Featherstone, *The Incomparable Christ*, Deseret Book, SLC, 1996.

10. Mayo Clinic Womens Healthsource, Boulder, Co. Vol. 3#3 and Vol. 3#7 1999.

11. THE FAMILY: A Proclamation to the World, The Church of Jesus Christ of Latter-Day Saints, 1995.

12. The Parent Institute, Parents Make a Difference Newsletter, Fairfax Station, Virginia, April, 1998 vol.9 #8.

13. AMCAP, Association of Mormon Counselors and Psychotherapists Conference, SLC, UT. April 1999, speaker F.Covey.

14. Dunn and Hargett Inc., Growing Together Newsletter, Lafayette, Indiana, 1993.

15. The Parent Institute, Parents Make a Difference Newsletter, Fairfax Station, Virginia, 1993.

16. J. Chamberlain, *Eliminate Your SDB's* (Self-Defeating

Behaviors), BYU Press, Provo, Utah, 1978.

17. T.A. Rando, *Grief, Dying and Death,* Research Press co., Champaign, IL., 1984.

18. Doka, K.J. & J.D. Morgan, (Eds.).(1993), *Death and Spirituality*, Amityville, NY: Baywood

19. Thibodeau, S.M. (1988). Sibling response to chronic illness: The role of the clinical nurse specialist. *Issues in Comprehensive Nursing*, 11, 17-28.

Chapter 13

1. Joe Bayly, TCF Carroltton-Farmers Branch, TX July Newsletter p. 3.

2. M.Dickson, Grief Seminars, Dallas, Texas 1992.

Index

About the Authors

Dennis and Joyce Ashton

The Ashtons are the parents of six children, four of whom are living. They enjoy many grandchildren.

Joyce is a registered nurse. She works for Rocky Mountain Hospice as a Spiritual and Bereavement Advisor. She has served as a teacher/counselor in Relief Society, Young Women and Primary, and served several years as a Ward and Stake Young Women's President.

Dennis has worked with LDS Family Services since 1972. He has a Masters Degree in clinical Social Work and is a Board Certified Licensed Psychotherapist. Dennis is a former AMCAP board member and has served as a Sunday School teacher, High Priest group leader, Bishop, High Councilman, ward and stake Young Mens President, and temple worker.

This is the third work about grief and healing methods that the Ashtons have authored together.

CEDAR FORT, INCORPORATED
Order Form

Name:_____

Address: _____

City: _____ State: _____ Zip: _____

Phone: (   ) _____ Daytime phone: (   ) _____

Jesus Wept

Quantity: _____ @ $14.95 each: _____

plus $3.49 shipping & handling for the first book: _____

(add 99¢ shipping for each additional book)

Utah residents add 6.25% for state sales tax: _____

TOTAL: _____

Bulk purchasing, shipping and handling quotes available upon request.

Please make check or money order payable to:

Cedar Fort, Incorporated.

Mail this form and payment to:

Cedar Fort, Inc.

925 North Main St.

Springville, UT 84663

You can also order on our website **www.cedarfort.com**
or e-mail us at sales@cedarfort.com or call 1-800-SKYBOOK